GETTING INTO

Retailing

FIRST EDITION

JOANNA GRIGG

TROTMAN

Getting into Retailing
This first edition published in 2002 by Trotman and Company Ltd
2 The Green, Richmond, Surrey TW9 1PL

© Joanna Grigg 2002

The right of Joanna Grigg to be identified as the author of this work has been
asserted by her in accordance with the Copyright, Designs and Patents Act 1988.

British Library Cataloguing in Publication Data
A catalogue record for this book is available from the
British Library.

ISBN 0 85660 830 0

Typeset by Palimpsest Book Production Limited,
Polmont, Stirlingshire

Printed and bound in Great Britain
by Creative Print & Design (Wales) Ltd

CONTENTS

ABOUT THE AUTHOR

Before becoming a specialist careers author and trainer Joanna Grigg spent many years working part-time in retail environments. She loved the customer contact and the whole atmosphere.

Between then and now she graduated from university and has worked in accountancy, sales, publishing, teaching and the community. Her own children now deliver newspapers and serve customers in shops; perhaps one of them will read this book and go into the exciting world of retailing.

ACKNOWLEDGEMENTS

I'd like to thank the people who spoke to me about their work, either informally or by arrangement with their employer. It was good to meet you and to explore your different workplaces. I'd also like to thank the people in head offices who spent time finding suitable people for me to speak with, and who gave me so much background information.

Joanna Grigg, June 2002

INTRODUCTION

When you're looking for career ideas, think about an industry that:

- has many different types of work
- is geared up for young people but encourages older people
- allows you to travel, to train, qualify and progress fast, based on your own ability and commitment
- is an integral part of the day-to-day lives of everyone in this country.

This describes retailing, of course. Whether you're thinking of leaving school after GCSEs or A-levels, are at university or have experience of other work, retailing offers many and increasing opportunities. This book offers an introduction to one of the fastest-moving work areas with the broadest of entry qualifications and career opportunities once you're in. It's certainly worth thinking about.

WHAT IS RETAILING?

Retailing (or 'retail'), along with wholesaling, forms what are known as the 'distributive industries' – the parts of our economy that get the goods to the people. Although this book concentrates on retailing, there is a short section on wholesaling (see page 76).

Retailing is what happens in shops (and some other workplaces): it's the process of selling goods to customers (see the next chapter for a fuller definition). And although this may seem to be a simple process, there are many elements to it that the ordinary shopper never sees or thinks about. Even on the shop floor, there are things going on that perhaps you've never noticed:

- stocktaking (seeing how much is on the shelves)
- shelf filling
- cashing-up tills
- activities involving training

1

- display staff arranging goods in the window or on display units
- customer service staff sorting out customer queries
- managers watching, assessing, supervising
- personal shoppers helping individuals to find what they want . . . the list goes on and on.

Add to this the behind-the-scenes work and it's a massive operation. The retailing industry:

- employs more than a tenth of the British workforce: one in every nine working adults, 3 million people, making it the UK's largest industry
- generates an annual turnover of over £200 billion, with every UK family spending an average of £144 per week through retailers
- created 58,400 new jobs in 2001, which was 22% of all new jobs.

For an idea of what actually goes on, whether in full view of the customer, behind the scenes, at head office or somewhere on a motorway, have a look at the next two chapters in Part One: the Retailing Industry (page 7) and What's the Work Like? (page 13) for a realistic glance at how it might feel to work in retail.

Types of work

There are sales jobs, which vary in the degree to which you need to persuade the customer to buy (rather than simply taking the money), customer support roles, and others such as those described above. There are also many background and support roles (in head office and branches) such as merchandising, buying, display, accountancy, marketing, and so on. These work roles are described, along with profiles of people doing them, in Part Two, starting on page 32.

CURRENT TRENDS IN RETAILING

At the time of writing (mid 2002), retailing equals profit, expansion and success. We are in a 'boom' period, and even though experts have predicted recession, customers carrying on shopping have, to a large extent, averted this threat.

During recessions, people have less money to spend on consumer goods and even the essentials often get whittled down. When people lose their jobs, for instance, their weekly grocery trolley contains less. Retailers who have planned for the inevitable swings in economic activity will weather the storms. It's those who make the wrong predictions that sometimes fail. So, successful retailing demands a large element of predicting the economy, as well as predicting trends in fashion, home goods, foods, etc:

- what will people want to be buying in six or twelve months' time?
- how much money will they have?
- what environment will they want to be shopping in?
- how plush should the shop furnishings be to attract the 'right' sort of customer? And so on.

Successful retailers survive the storms and come out stronger for it. The giants, such as Marks and Spencer, which has taken a market bashing recently but now looks on-the-up, need to adapt to survive. And so do smaller retailers, whose margins for error may be smaller and also need to keep customers rolling in and buying.

Many of these observations apply to other industries, too. But of all the places to work, retailing seems to be more constantly adapting. Retailers need to make their operations more efficient and increase profits, and to do this many diversify, selling a wider range of goods than before. Think of shops that started out selling one type of goods and now sell several, for example, fashion retailers that also sell insurance. The high street is full of evidence of retailing trends: more coffee bars is an unmissable one.

What's this saying about our shopping habits? It says that nowadays, we like to make an occasion of shopping, that it's becoming more of a social event and leisure activity. And what are retailers doing to adapt to this trend? Making shops more pleasant places to spend time, drawing customers into their own coffee shops and restaurants, advertising lifestyle elements to their goods even though these weren't obvious before. This is all about attracting customers and inducing them to buy. This latter element is vital – window-shoppers may fill towns and shopping arcades, making places seem to thrive, but they need to be converted into actual shoppers.

There are other major changes taking place in retailing. As well as changes related to the economy, current trends include:

- Retail parks (out-of-town centres for large retailers) are still growing where planners allow them
- Growth can be seen in the high street (particularly, but not exclusively, in areas where planners limit the 'greenfield' retailing parks, above), though it's mainly larger retailers investing here. Smaller shops may thrive in specialist areas of town, or these smaller units may be converted into offices, flats, townhouses or coffee bars
- Discount retailing is a big growth area, sometimes integrated into the retail park concept with designer discount centres, for instance
- 'Clicks and mortar' is also growing – this means using the Internet to buy items you might otherwise find in shops. This contradicts the idea of shopping as a leisure pursuit, however. Analysts are interested to see how far we'll be happy to shop from home, and whether older people are prepared to change their ways in line with the new technologies
- We now buy some of our food via the Internet – how far will we go with this?
- Technology is having a huge impact generally within retailing, so even if sales don't continue to grow at such a rate in 'e-tailing', as above, new technology is making all areas more efficient
- Mail order is generally a growth area, whether ordered online or by post or telephone. Call centres are growing, which allow shoppers to order goods and also give customers the service that would be available face-to-face in a shop and is still necessary for some shoppers
- The growth of 'e-tailing' and mail order can mean the demise of shops in certain areas where they don't get enough custom – these are often rural and disadvantaged areas. Government policy is looking at ways to prevent increasing social exclusion through these shoppers being unable to access the goods they need
- DIY, gardening and other home retailers are having a bonanza
- Look for yourself – the trends are visible on the high street and elsewhere, as well as within your PC – try the websites of organisations listed in Further Information (page 84) to stay in touch.

WORKING IN RETAILING

More variety means that new and diverse skills are needed by people working in retailing. Computerised systems mean that less time is spent in traditional roles, such as at the till and in the stock room. Numbers employed in retailing are still expected to increase, but roles will change according to the needs of the new technologies and systems.

As you research this area of work, think not only of what you see now in the high street or within your computer, but also where retailing is likely to be going over the next years. Think what mixes of skills will be in demand, and where you are most likely to be able to gain those skills. Current work areas are described in Part Two of this book: ensure your research covers reading and asking about where the industry is going next. For research ideas, look at the section Further Information, starting on page 84.

In the meantime, the best way to research it is to do it: as the chapter Getting into Retailing (page 78) describes, the best start is to get some retail experience: it's available on any high street – all you have to do is ask!

PART ONE:
About retailing, about you

Chapter 1
THE RETAILING INDUSTRY

THE STRUCTURE OF RETAILING

Some definitions:

- Retailing involves moving goods from the point of production or from a wholesaler to the point where they're sold to the final customer (usually in shops), and then finally selling them to the customer. This sounds straightforward but there are many different processes that the goods go through, each of which requires a range of different people and systems.
- Wholesaling involves buying goods from suppliers (these suppliers may be the people who make them, or importers, or other wholesalers) then selling them on to retailers, or to organisations that need them for other reasons (such as those using them to make their own products).
- The 'supply chain' is the term used to describe the whole process whereby goods are moved from production to the final consumer (shopper). All the goods you buy have travelled along this supply chain, and people who work in retailing are an essential part of it. To understand retailing it's important to be able to 'see' the supply chain clearly, because the people and processes involved in each part of it affect all the other parts.

Here is an overview of the supply chain and some of the people involved:

Stage	Process	Some of the people involved
Production	The manufacturing of goods that are expected to satisfy the demands of customers	Designers; scientists; engineers; health and safety experts; retailers for feedback, etc.
Buying	Shops only stock certain ranges – expert buyers choose these and negotiate price, quantity, colour etc.	Suppliers; buyers; merchandisers; strategists; accountants; scientists and technologists
Distribution	Goods must be stored then distributed. Warehouses receive large quantities of goods and divide these up, repackaging into smaller quantities as required. They then send them on as ordered	Warehousing and distribution staff; network designers; transport staff
Arrival of goods	Goods arrive in the shops and need to be unpacked, stored then displayed	Stockroom staff; display staff
Sales	Shelves need to be filled to look good, then items are sold to customers	Stockroom work; sales staff; customer service, and many, many more roles; management with responsibility overall for profitability

(For more information on the roles mentioned in the final column above, look in Part Two, Types of Work, page 32.)

From this table outlining the supply chain you can see that there's more to buying an item than a quick visit to a shop. Each of the stages described involves the collaboration of others elsewhere in the chain and systems that allow staff to operate the chain efficiently. Though some roles are mentioned above, there are in fact many different specialist areas. When you think how many different specialists there are even among sales staff within shops, extrapolate this to the entire chain and you have thousands of slightly different roles. When you're entering retailing your knowledge and skills are limited, but as you learn you'll come to understand more about the roles within your particular part of the industry. It's often then that people start to specialise.

TYPES OF EMPLOYER

Very broadly, the industry can be divided into these main types of organisation, classified by ownership and size rather than by product or level of service:

Multiple retailers, operating 'chains' of stores.

■ These chains are usually specialised into one sector of goods for sale, such as electrical, food, home, fashion and so on
■ Many of the larger chains liaise with suppliers to produce 'own brand' products
■ They may also run their own warehousing and distribution, so they offer a wider range of careers than some smaller multiples or independents which obtain stock direct from outside organisations
■ Careers include specialist head office roles such as work with information and communications technology, research, scientific and technical roles, as well as roles within distribution
■ They also offer plenty of management possibilities through larger training schemes and more stores to move to for promotion opportunities.

Department stores sell a range of goods within one store rather than specialising like the 'multiples'.

■ They can be single stores, or chains. Some of the single stores are actually owned by larger groups even when they keep their own identities

- They generally offer a greater degree of sales service than other types of store, and customers often have great loyalty to one particular store for all their needs (sometimes, though not usually, including food shopping)
- Stores are organised into specialist departments and each department offers chances for career progression. As well as this, it's possible to move from one department to another and so gain a wide range of experience
- Department stores offer similar head office and regional roles and opportunities to those in the 'multiples'.

Independent retailers are single stores, or sometimes small chains, usually privately owned.

- These may be unusual specialist shops, or perhaps grocery or fresh food outlets. As they're smaller they can give first-hand experience of the whole range of retail activities if you get on well. They may be owner-managed, with perhaps less chance of career progression
- They offer similar work to the smaller chain stores: buying, merchandising, display, customer service and sales.

Mail order companies despatch goods directly to individual customers.

- These are the catalogue and Internet retailers
- They have warehouses and distribution centres but no stores
- They offer careers in science and technology, buying and merchandising, and warehousing. Many offer telephone sales and customer service work. These companies also offer specialist design work in catalogue and website publishing.

Cooperatives are owned by the people who work for them.

- All workers receive a share of the profits each year as well as having a say in how their organisation is run
- There are very many smaller cooperatives, often in food and dairy retailing, as well as 'multiples' (chain stores).

These definitions don't take type of goods, or location, into account. These aspects become more obvious when looking at workplaces, below:

WORKPLACES

You already know that retailers work in:

- high street stores – 'multiples', independents, department stores
- shopping malls within the high street
- out-of-town shopping malls or retail parks
- supermarkets/hypermarkets
- corner shops and small clusters of shops.

There are other places which may not be so obvious:

- airports, ports or other travel locations
- ferries, planes, trains
- markets
- head offices
- regional offices
- call centres
- Internet call centres/depots
- on the road (travelling) as a buyer or manager
- laboratories, liaising with design
- factory or production centres, liaising with production
- warehouses
- at home – some managers and buyers, for instance, are based at home though they travel extensively.

The Distributive National Training Organisation (DNTO) (see Further Information, page 85 for more information) lists these examples of typical working environments:

- Fast food stores
- Food supermarkets
- Department stores
- Electronics goods stores
- Clothing and fashion outlets
- Telecommunications stores
- Hardware shops
- Newsagents
- Sports suppliers
- Florists
- Gift and card shops

- Cash and carry stores
- DIY shops
- Catalogue stores
- Transport companies
- Warehouses and many, many more.

One way to get a 'feel' for different types of organisations, environments and locations is to look at the recruitment websites or brochures of the larger retailers. Reading their information and comparing one with another will give you some of the flavour of the work and the organisations. Remember that they are trying to 'sell' you the idea of working for them, so everything is portrayed in a positive light. Then go into the stores themselves and see how they compare. Think about whether you'd like to work there, for that type of organisation, in that sized store, etc.

You can find recruitment brochures in your careers office or centre, or go on the Internet and search, then email your request. Websites are available through search engines. Try starting at the members page of the British Institute of Retailing (BIR), which has links to some of the larger retailers. See Further Information, page 84, for website URLs.

Chapter 2
WHAT'S THE WORK LIKE?

Here's a selection of retailing people talking about their work:

'I've never worked so hard.' (pharmacy supervisor)

'I didn't think I'd get used to it but I did, surprisingly fast. Now I look at new trainees and they can hardly stand up all day, they're used to sitting in lessons. It's a big shock. But it's interesting so they put up with the first few weeks. You get fit really fast, then it's easier.' (department store departmental manager)

'I hated it. I hated filling shelves and the stock room was a filthy nightmare. I couldn't wait to leave. I only lasted three weeks.' (school-leaver who dropped out of a retail scheme and is now back in education)

'It was tough but I liked the people and the customers. I liked being polite to the rude ones and turning them around so they were happy. You've got to like people, if you're not interested in people then there's no point.' (graduate trainee in electrical store)

'I've always loved shopping, now I help people do it all day and I still love it.' (fashion sales assistant)

Because retailing is such a massive industry there's no one answer to the question 'what's it like?' The work is certainly different from its old-fashioned image of an owner-shopkeeper on the street corner offering a wide range of foods or household goods. These shops still exist (though many of them have been 'squeezed out' economically by more efficient, larger chains of retailers) and they form one end of a vast work spectrum. At the other end you might have a call-centre, where you sit at an office workstation and take telephone calls from customers who want to order goods from a catalogue.

In between these two extremes, the high street has expanded to include huge 'multiples', department stores, specialists and generalists. Out-of-town areas have evolved as retail parks. Markets have grown and changed.

Equally, you might work with small goods such as toiletries, or with larger, less frequent purchases such as furniture. When you're selling, you'll approach customers differently according to the goods and the type of customer. If you're advertising the goods, or accounting for them, your approach will vary here too. These various environments result in different work experiences.

As well as the variety in size and type of organisation, the goods it sells, how, and where, there's the chance to set up your own shop, stall or website and go into business as a retailer.

Here are some points about retailing that stretch across the whole industry:

- It's a fast-moving industry, where products, ideas and people don't stay still very long
- You'll wear a uniform or need to dress and present yourself well. This may mean a trendy appearance to suit the store. Warehouse staff usually wear uniforms – they need tough clothes as well as a strong image and identity. Specialist workers need specialist clothing, such as workers in fast food outlets using hairnets or caps
- It's physically demanding, and you need to be fit to cope with being on your feet all day, walking and carrying, or just standing talking to people
- The opposite extreme is checkout work, where you'll be seated for long periods of time, though your employer should give you regular breaks. This can be tedious work and most people entering retailing will spend some time doing some junior or lower level work such as this. You need to find ways of making the work interesting: taking interest in your customers is essential here
- With increasing store opening hours you'll find yourself working odd hours, and often long hours too. Weekend working is fairly standard, often including Sundays
- You'll also need to work at times when you could do with a rest. At Christmas, for instance, you'll work really hard up to the final closing time, but then the sales start soon after Christmas and these need to be prepared for. You may find there's little time to be with your family at festivals like these, and little flexibility for other holiday times .

- Similarly, you need to be flexible in where you live as, to get the best promotions and a wide range of experience, you may need to move stores. This is vital for graduate trainees, though some employers will let you remain within a region. School-leavers or the less ambitious may not need this flexibility.

When asked to sum up 'retailing as a career' one graduate trainee said:

'It's fast, really fast. I never stop still, and as soon as I've learnt something, I move on to the next thing. It's hard work, but it's exciting, demanding, and never stops. I love that.'

Chapter 3
PERSONAL CHARACTERISTICS YOU NEED

Retailing is an industry that's about personality as much as it is about qualifications – sometimes, it's all down to personality. Words that come to mind when thinking about retailers are 'young', 'dynamic', 'ambitious'. This doesn't preclude older people, however, or the less 'bubbly' and driven (for information about the 'age' aspect, see below, and for details of qualifications see the next chapter, on page 19). But you do need certain personality traits and a willingness and enthusiasm to carry you along. Broadly, to succeed at any level in retailing you need to be:

- a fast learner
- a good administrator
- a good listener
- able to communicate effectively and in a friendly way
- able to get on with all types of people
- approachable
- calm
- cheerful and friendly
- committed to customer service – meaning that the customer must leave the shop happy
- courteous
- enthusiastic
- fit – there's a lot of walking, standing and sometimes lifting and other physical activities. You also need plenty of stamina
- happy to work long and antisocial hours when required
- helpful
- literate and numerate
- patient
- self-confident
- smartly dressed (possibly in a uniform)
- willing to learn.

In addition, if you're ambitious and want to get on within retailing, you'll need to be:

- a good organiser
- able to see the funny side of things
- able to work in a team
- adaptable, able to work in different kinds of environments, as needed
- creative, and able to think through problems imaginatively
- driven
- lively
- logical
- looking for promotion and to be a leader, and have the qualities that make you a good leader
- professional in your attitude to work and people
- responsible, and keen to seek responsibility
- self-motivated
- willing to relocate as the job requires.

These characteristics indicate an ideal person – clearly no one is going to be superb at everything. You'll learn many skills and abilities as you progress. Looking down the list, there are many related characteristics that draw a picture of an outgoing, positive person. If you recognise this person as you, in essence at least, then perhaps retailing is for you. If, however, you'd rather have your eyes on a list of accounting figures, preferring not to speak to anyone about them (or similar, introverted tasks) then perhaps you should think again.

In addition to the general skills and attributes listed above, the various specialist roles require specialist skills: these are outlined in the relevant section of Part Two.

AGE

Retailing is a fast, energetic environment to work in and young people are especially suited to it. However, many companies now encourage older people to join them. Recently publicised examples include B&Q, the DIY chain, which positively attracts older people. This was initially because they foresaw a lack of young people coming through as demographics changed. It has found that older people make good employees for a number of reasons: they take less sick leave, they are more punctual, they understand people better and therefore relate better to customers, they have their own life and DIY experience to draw on, and so on.

The John Lewis Partnership offers all employees (called 'partners') six months' paid leave after 25 years' service, and this is often taken: clearly, these people are no longer spring chickens and have remained with the company for over half their working lives.

So some retailers like, and take care of, their older employees despite the young image of the industry generally. Whether older people can forge successful 'second careers' as late entrants is another matter – are employers willing to invest in them in terms of training and career opportunities? Most entrants into retail management schemes are in their 20s. Older people who want to move up within retail management need a retailing or other organisational background, and to have proven skills in relevant areas. The best route if you're older and don't have this experience could be to join a retailer at a lower level and show particular ability and commitment. You might initiate some distance learning of your own, such as courses run by the British Shops and Stores Association (BSSA) or the Institute of Sales and Marketing Management (ISMM). Management should then consider you for training and promotion.

Chapter 4
QUALIFICATIONS YOU NEED

You can go into retailing with no qualifications at all, with GCSEs, A-Levels or a degree. All employers, whatever level you're entering at, will want you to be literate and numerate. This usually means a basic spread of GCSEs grades A-C, including Maths and English. Small local retailers may employ you without any qualifications if you can convince them, and then go on to prove yourself. After all, sales is about personality. And of course, you can go into business as a retailer later on without any academic qualifications. You still need to be literate and numerate, though.

Going straight from school, sixth form or further education college

- There are no formal entry requirements to work within retailing, though larger employers often look for at least two GCSEs at grade C and above. You may be asked to sit a test in Maths and English when you apply. You'll need a good sprinkling of GCSEs if you want to progress in any career – and even if you can talk your way around this when you first start in your local branch, you may find later that you can't progress as far as you want without these, or without A-levels or a degree. Employers vary here. Some encourage their staff to carry on gaining qualifications, and may pay for you to do this, and give you study-leave. Find out when researching on the Internet/at the careers office, and ask at interview
- Starting as a sales assistant is your best bet if you don't have many qualifications. Then, if you're good, you'll be spotted, trained and will be able to progress
- However, the best thing is to have as many qualifications as possible, as this keeps more options open now and in the future.

Government training schemes

- If you're aged 16–24 you might enter retailing as a Modern Apprentice (for details of these see the section on training, page 25). There are two levels: Foundation Modern Apprentice (FMA) and Advanced Modern Apprentice (AMA). They both lead to NVQ/SVQ qualifications (these are National Vocational Qualifications and Scottish Vocational Qualifications, see the chapter on training for more details, page 24). You'll need certain educational qualifications for entry, which vary and are agreed by the employer and the training organisation. For the AMA they are generally a minimum of five GCSEs at grades A–C, fewer for the FMA. (The FMA often leads onto an AMA.) Getting onto a Modern Apprenticeship can be competitive as places are limited, so it's worth applying early. These are run through the Skillseekers scheme in Scotland (see p. 25 for details).

Going into management training

- All larger retailers look for management trainees and they generally take people from university or after a few years' work experience in another industry. Some select their future managers from people who entered as sales assistants and have shown aptitude. However, these people mostly have at least two A-levels.
- You'll need at least a second class degree if entering as a graduate, and possibly an upper second class degree (2.1) or above. The discipline doesn't matter unless you're going into a specific area such as finance, which requires related study, or technical sales – an expanding area when you'll need to have studied at university in that specific discipline. Some recruiters have other specific needs – see their recruitment literature.

Display work

This is more art-based, and you'll need a GCSE in art, as well as English and possibly Maths. You also need to show further interest, such as A-level and possibly a degree in Art and Design. There are specific qualifications such as Technician and General Certificates for people who don't want to study for a degree. For more information on these contact the British Display Society or see their website (see page 87 for details).

Specialist roles such as merchandising and buying

You may go into these areas after experience in retail management, in which case you'll need the qualifications listed above under management trainees. Some recruiters will take you straight into specialist training. More information on specific roles and entry requirements is in the relevant section of Part Two.

Other roles

For certain roles, you'll need to gain a degree in that area first. This could include finance, technical sales, Information Technology (IT) or other support roles. A degree in a business-related subject will qualify you to enter as a management trainee, or to enter more specific areas such as human resources. You may specialise in one area such as this during your degree course.

Retailing degrees

It's possible to study retailing-related subjects at university. Although most graduate management training schemes in retailing don't ask for specific degree disciplines when you apply, you may still want to specialise early in this way. Examples include studying Purchasing and Supply Chain Management, or Retail Management. Look on the UCAS (Universities and Colleges Admissions Service) website for details of all courses. The British Institute of Retailing website lists universities and colleges offering retail degree courses and other qualifications recognised by the industry. For website URLs see Further Information, page 84.

Postgraduate study

You can remain at university after your first degree, and take, perhaps, an MSc in Logistics or MA in Marketing. These can be useful in getting a training place with one of the blue chip (very large) retailers where places are greatly in demand.

Qualifications once you're in retailing

You should gain NVQ/SVQs in appropriate subjects as you train with your new employer. These will be at different levels depending on your entry level and abilities. There is currently a big push towards workers gaining their basic skills qualifications, aimed at those who entered work with minimal literacy, numeracy, communication and IT skills. But retailing is an industry where it's possible to work towards and gain NVQ/SVQs at level 4 (Managerial level) whatever level you start at, and professional qualifications (NVQ/SVQ level 5) beyond that. Research this with the employers you're interested in. See the chapter on training for more details (page 23).

Chapter 5
TRAINING

This chapter looks at training within the retailing industry and gives an overview of what's available. When you're doing your own research you can add to this with specific information about employers' training schemes, or perhaps about more specialist functions within the industry such as display work.

Once you're working in retailing, your employer will train you.

■ If you're starting with a Saturday job, this may be informal on-the-job training such as showing you how to fill the shelves or work the till

■ Even then, your basic training should also cover issues such as health and safety: making sure you know how to get out of the building in an emergency; how to work without endangering yourself and others, and similar issues.

When you go into a job as the first part of your retailing career, you can get into training in a bigger way.

■ Think ahead to what you might be doing in a year from now, or five years from now, and what training you need to ensure that you will be doing just that

■ Your plans may well change but going into work without getting the best possible training is short-sighted.

Most employers are geared up to training, already having schemes running that you should be able to slot into.

■ Do ensure that this is the case

■ With smaller employers there's been less emphasis on training and gaining NVQs/SVQs (see below), but these days even smaller employers are being encouraged to train their staff in basic then more advanced skills. It helps the employers as well as the industry as a whole.

■ If your employer isn't so keen, do some research of your own and suggest ways in which you can work towards an NVQ/SVQ while doing your job.

- There are plenty of websites with this information. See Further Information for website ideas (page 84).

WHAT ARE NVQs/SVQs?

These are National Vocational Qualifications and Scottish Vocational Qualifications. They are a measure of your competence at work. You can't get them at school though you can get them through college courses that are vocational and practical-based. They are used throughout work as a measure of your expertise. You can get them all through your working life, and you can work towards NVQ/SVQs at different levels.

They aren't academic qualifications (such as you get at school) so it's not really sensible to compare them to these, but people do. If you want a rough comparison of levels, they are:

NVQ/SVQ Level 1 – roughly equivalent to GCSE at grades D and below
NVQ/SVQ Level 2 – roughly equivalent to GCSE at grades A-C
NVQ/SVQ Level 3 – roughly equivalent to A-level

Levels 4 and 5 are managerial and professional grades, which you would move on to after plenty of experience. There are four levels of NVQ/SVQ awarded within the retailing industry. These levels are:

Level 1   Level 1 Distribution NVQ/SVQ, basic: for new staff
Level 2   Retail NVQ/SVQ, for staff who can work unsupervised
Level 3   Retail NVQ/SVQ, supervisory level for team leaders
Level 4   Retail NVQ/SVQ, department/store management level

Managers can then work towards a general NVQ/SVQ Level 5 in management even though there is no specific retailing qualification at this level.

How do NVQs/SVQs fit into your training?

Every industry uses the NVQ/SVQ system for its training. Although each industry has its own NTO (National Training Organisations, now becoming Sector Skills Councils (SSCs)), once you have an NVQ/SVQ in customer service skills from working in retailing, for instance, you can use this in another industry that requires these skills. Some skills are very industry-specific, whilst others are shared between many industries. Management and sales skills are more easily transferred between industries than mechanical and other technical skills, for instance. So retailing is a good industry to train in even if you're not sure that you want to stay in it forever, as many of its skills are transferable.

But when you start training in retailing you need to be committed, for a certain length of time at least. NVQ/SVQ training qualifications may take one to three years to achieve – and sometimes longer than this.

WHAT TRAINING SCHEMES ARE AVAILABLE?

Most young people entering retailing go in straight after school, after university or in the following few years. School leavers often enter Modern Apprenticeships, while most graduates go into management training schemes (see below).

Advanced Modern Apprenticeships (AMAs)/Skillseekers in Scotland

These are training schemes set up by your employer in discussion and with support from government organisations known as the LSC (Learning and Skills Council) in England and Wales, LEC (Local Enterprise Company) in Scotland, or T and EA (Training and Enterprise Agency) in Northern Ireland. They're set up for motivated and able young people who hope to progress into supervisory or management levels. You need to be aged between 16 and 24 and complete the training by your 25th birthday. The training is flexible, and some people complete it faster than others, but generally it's estimated that it'll take you about three years. You work towards NVQs/SVQs at levels 2 then 3, possibly in Retail Operations or in Distribution and Warehousing. But because retailing needs so many skills that are transferable between industries, you may work towards NVQs/SVQs that are less industry-specific, such as customer care or IT.

You'll have a written training agreement, work in a retail or warehouse environment and go to college or a training centre for a day or evening a week, perhaps, as well as receiving on-the-job training and formal, off-the-job in-house training if you work for a larger employer.

Foundation Modern Apprenticeships (FMAs, formerly National Traineeships)

These start at a lower level than AMAs and once completed may take you onto an AMA scheme. They are run in the same way and in collaboration with the same agencies. They lead towards NVQs/SVQs at level 2.

Modern Apprenticeships generally

Both sets of Modern Apprenticeships/Skillseekers (AMAs and FMAs) offer a high quality training route, with plenty of training support and an assurance that your training needs will be taken seriously. You won't just be left to clear out the stockroom day in, day out, though of course, starting at ground level in any industry does require you to gain experience of all aspects of the work. Showing you're willing to 'get your hands dirty' and work hard will pay dividends in this training environment, and promotion can be rapid for the right people.

Both AMAs and FMAs are available in either Retail, or Distribution and Warehousing.

Management training schemes

All the larger retailers need to train people to run their stores. They are looking for a mix of personal characteristics that fits the industry generally and their own philosophy in particular, as well as a good academic record leading to a degree or HND. Although it's possible to get onto management training schemes without a degree/HND, perhaps by being 'spotted' after your AMA, the fast-track schemes all require this.

The best way to research this, and the particular needs of recruiters, is to search on the Internet or at your careers service. Some employers produce brochures to attract graduate applicants, others have all their information online. Some prefer you to apply online while others want a paper application or a call to head office.

As a rule, graduate schemes offer:

- fast-track training into store management roles, sometimes within a year, though perhaps after two to four years
- the term 'store management' could mean running a small high street store, or being second-in-command in a larger one
- within another short time period you could be in sole charge of a huge store, or perhaps manage a group of stores
- after this you might specialise, perhaps into merchandising or buying, though some employers train you in these roles from scratch
- or you might remain in store management and take on greater responsibility, perhaps becoming a director.

If you do well, you really can progress extremely fast. It's hard work though. You'll need to:

- be genuinely interested in the products you sell, and in the whole retailing industry
- commit yourself to your training and to the organisation, being prepared to help out at short notice and to work antisocial hours
- attend courses, in-house or residential, as well as learning on-the-job
- relate to people at all levels, including long-established teams of older sales assistants and supervisors who may not be too happy with a cocky youngster coming in and telling them what to do. You need excellent interpersonal skills, and an ability to motivate a team and work as a part of it as well as to lead from the front
- relocate to take up new challenges, though if you can't do this, many employers are happy for you to remain within a region. They probably won't be able to promote you as fast, though
- learn skills in a variety of areas, because as a general manager (rather than as a specialist) you need to understand the various functions, such as accounts, IT, distribution, buying and so on, and pull them all together
- be responsible for the profitability of your store, and make changes as necessary to ensure this increases
- have lots of new ideas and be able to put them effectively into practice.

Training schemes in specific areas of retailing

Most larger retailers also offer graduate training in specific areas of the industry, such as finance, IT, distribution, display, buying, merchandising and so on. You may need a relevant degree. For instance, in finance you'll need a maths, finance or numerical degree of some sort, and in IT you'll need a degree in an IT discipline.

Training schemes are designed to give you the required knowledge of the industry and the function, as well as, often, a professional qualification. In finance, you'll probably be offered training towards gaining the CIMA qualification. This may 'slow you up' compared to retail management trainees, but not much. Your experience and qualifications will allow you to move fast to the top if you're able and committed. Again, graduate brochures or websites tell you more about these schemes.

You may be able to train in these areas after entering the industry as a school leaver. You'll need to show promise, and prove yourself over a longer time period, but the industry is hungry for good, motivated people so there are real possibilities. It is, however, simpler to go in as a graduate trainee as the scheme is set up and waiting for you. Whichever route you take, you'll gain experience on the shop floor so that you understand the sales function and the teamwork involved, and will probably work in all the departments to gain enough experience to understand how the various functions work.

Some functions, such as display, are less graduate-orientated in some areas of the industry, while others require an art or design degree. Again, research the possibilities through the Internet and the careers service. See the various sections of Part Two (starting on page 32) for role-specific information.

Ongoing training

There's now an accreditation scheme for retail managers, run by the British Institute of Retailing (BIR). You may also work towards NVQs/SVQs in management or towards a professional qualification, perhaps later in your career rather than as a new graduate. New degree courses are being devised which allow retail managers to gain qualifications, such as a BSc in Work-Based Retail Management at Surrey University. So although retailing used to be an industry where you went in young, worked hard and progressed informally, now it's becoming more structured with more formal qualifications on offer and many chances to learn and formalise that learning as you progress.

Further research for specific types of retailing

If you're interested in specific areas of retailing such as bookselling or food, contact the relevant professional organisation for specific training opportunities and needs. Your careers adviser will help you with this, or you can search on the Internet. Some contact points are listed in Further Information (page 84).

Chapter 6
SALARIES AND OTHER BENEFITS

Retailing used to be considered a relatively poorly paid industry but since the advent of the minimum wage and faster promotion opportunities, it's now more competitive with other areas of work. Some retailers earn very well indeed, while those on lower salaries find that other perks can make a difference to their basic wage.

Pay levels vary depending on the size of employer, the type of employer and the location. For more precise information ask at your careers centre or Jobcentre for local pay rates. If you're part of a management structure then you will be moving around the country and your employer should ensure that your pay reflects the local situations and your needs.

PAY

Entry-level pay

The minimum wage (see below) is designed to ensure that all workers receive a living wage. Many employers set this as their entry-level wage, though some pay more than this and it should rise in cities. You should earn more for working Sundays and other antisocial shifts, and be paid for overtime worked. There may also be commission, which can add substantially to your pay.

Minimum wage levels (from October 2002):

Main (adult) rate for workers aged 22 and over	£4.20 an hour
Development rate for workers aged 18–21 inclusive	£3.60 an hour

(The minimum wage doesn't apply to workers under 18. Those 22 or over may receive the development rate during their first six months in a new job with a new employer or who are receiving accredited training.)

Management pay

Supervisors and managers can negotiate rises in their pay as they progress. Store managers should earn from £12,000 per annum, often substantially more than this. Managers don't generally receive overtime pay.

Graduate level entry

Employers are currently paying between £14–20,000 a year to new graduates entering management schemes. It's possible to be earning well in excess of £30,000 a year after five years.

COMMISSION AND OTHER BENEFITS

Many employers offer some form of commission scheme on sales, both on those you make yourself and on those of the store or group of stores. Managers will receive bonuses based on profitability; other staff may also be included in this type of scheme.

All employers offer discount schemes for their staff to buy goods at reduced prices. This can make a significant difference to your budget. There may be discounts available over a range of other stores within the same group. You may also get a company car once you're at management level, and certainly once you need a car for travelling for work. Pension, sickness, life assurance and other schemes generally improve with larger employers.

SPECIALIST ROLES

Pay for specialists within retailing, such as IT personnel and accountants, tends to follow the norms of those particular industries. Look at the specialist press for advertisements detailing earnings in particular roles and sectors.

PART TWO:
Types of work within retailing

Chapter 7
THE JOBS

BUYER

For many people this is 'the' place to be in retailing – it has a glamorous and exciting image. The work is indeed fast-moving at this 'cutting edge', where buyers take major decisions based on their experience, knowledge and intuition. It's also increasing in importance as retailing expands and becomes more complex. An organisation's profits are directly dependent on good buying decisions.

The work

Buyers place orders with wholesalers and manufacturers, sometimes ordering unique items to be made exclusively for their shops. You'll specialise in a certain area of retailing, such as men's fashions, motor parts or home furnishings. Over your career you might move from one specialist area to another.

Key elements of the job

- You need to know your 'customer profile' – the type of person who shops in your stores and what they are likely to want to buy
- You'll liaise with all your stores to discover what's selling and what the staff in the stores feel might sell well in future
- You'll find (source) products that you might want to buy. Researching these can be straightforward, as suppliers will approach you with

samples of goods and try to persuade you to buy them. But good buyers look further ahead than what's already in production or on offer, and this research can take you around the world to completely new sources

- You then decide which of these products your customers will want to buy, and how many they are likely to buy
- You also decide how much to pay for the goods and how much they should sell for in your stores
- You negotiate with suppliers on price, delivery, quantity and quality bearing in mind all your calculations, above
- In larger organisations you might take instructions from a senior buying committee, whereas in smaller operations you'll have more autonomy
- A buyer's role can be fairly narrow or very broad, depending on how the retail organisation is structured and run. It could include all sorts of policy decisions or might be more groundwork-based.

What's it like?

It's a highly responsible job as the whole retail operation depends on having the right goods in the shop at the right price. 'Right' in this context means having the goods that shoppers want and can afford to buy, and that will also make enough money in 'mark-up' (the difference between what you paid for them wholesale plus your transport costs, etc, and what you are selling them for, retail) to make the business viable.

Buying the wrong goods, buying them at the wrong price, or buying too few or too many, can make a retail business fail. It's highly competitive and fast-moving. You're judged by results, and you'll strive to better your own profits year on year. You'll be away from home visiting suppliers, exhibitions and shows, and then slot back into office life, then the next moment into store life. You'll build vital business relationships with suppliers, and need to keep these alive and positive. You may also run a team and need to train and motivate them. Because of the 'instinct' involved in buying decisions (a sense developed over years of analysing sales figures, speaking with store customers, suppliers, and colleagues, and watching trends emerge and develop, along with all the other elements of the role) you'll take risks – you'll see a range that you just 'feel' is going to work. This carries an exhilaration but also worry in case it doesn't sell. It's not for the faint-hearted.

Skills you need

You need to be:

- confident in your knowledge, choices and negotiating skills
- assertive
- interested in changing trends with an eye for style and fashions (in all areas, not just clothing) and a developed 'intuition' for the right thing
- analytical and objective
- numerate, and interested in financial patterns, with a good sense of business
- a good negotiator, communicator and decision-maker
- able to relate to a range of buyers and store staff
- happy to travel and work long hours. There can be a lot of foreign travel involved. You might be based at home, in head office or in a regional office or store.

Getting in

It's a job for people experienced in retail, though, increasingly, management training schemes recruit graduates to train as buying/merchandising assistants from the beginning. Others enter through general training or through sales work and later move across onto the buying function. However you start it will be years before you're making buying decisions on any scale, but once you've proved that you have the 'eye' for it, progress can be fast, based on the profits you bring to the organisation.

Buying and merchandising

Merchandising (which has its own section below) is an associated role. Different organisations divide the roles according to their needs and structure, often splitting them like this:

- Merchandisers are more involved in policy, and less involved with suppliers directly. They develop forecasts of sales and profits and work out the budgets that the buyers need to work to. Decisions about promotions and presentation are usually made by merchandisers, who are also responsible for the profits of their departments or stores

■ Buyers work more directly with suppliers, selecting from ranges of products already available and proposing new ones.

CASE STUDY

Sue is a menswear buyer for a national multiple. She has been in this role for four years after moving from assistant buyer in lingerie. 'Some people thought it strange that a woman took over the menswear, but that's not relevant: I developed a good eye for the ranges while I was in women's clothing and although I'm supplying men's clothing, in fact with our customers it's often the wives who do the shopping.

'I have to take account of variations across the country and ensure that I supply the right ranges – and sizes – to the right regions and stores within those regions. We don't go for 'trendy' but even so, some of our stores have slimmer, taller customers who want more up-to-date ranges and colours than others. It's vital to get that right.

'A lot of my time is spent on the phone, talking with assistant buyers and in meetings with colleagues. But sales figures are collated by computer these days so there's less faffing around with paperwork. But the bit I still like best, and the most important in my view, is researching new lines and supplier contact: getting what you want at the best price.'

Shahed, a fast food retailer, adds: 'Margins are very tight in food: I'm always looking at food costs and doing the sums. New suppliers approach me and ask me to switch to them. They often give good prices to begin with but I have to look at the longer term. Is my current supplier reliable and is the quality consistent? And is it worth trying a new supplier who might not be so good, just to save a few pounds now? Sometimes it's a difficult equation.'

CALL CENTRE WORK

Call centres are new workplaces which have been developing over the past decade or so, and now employ over a quarter of a million people who speak with customers over the phone. Not all call centres are part of the retailing industry but within those that are, call centre work is largely sales-based. There are also customer service, supervisory and management roles. See the job descriptions of these roles (in this section) for more information.

The work

Customers see catalogues, or perhaps advertisements on the Internet or on TV, and phone to order the goods they want. They may have a clear idea of what they want or may just be vaguely interested.

Staff in some call centres also make outgoing calls to potential customers, perhaps to people who have sent in forms to say that they're interested in being contacted, or perhaps to people on lists such as the telephone directory.

Key elements of the job

- As a sales adviser you'll talk with customers and advise them on aspects such as the type and size of goods
- You then persuade them to buy the goods
- You'll take their credit card details and enter them into the computer
- The computer then takes over, notifying the bank, the warehouse, and other parts of the business, about the order. The customer probably won't call back unless there's a problem, and then may not speak with you but to a customer service adviser
- You'll then move onto the next call
- Customer service adviser is another job title – the role may be more guidance than pure sales, though it can mean much the same thing. Other employers have varying job titles for their staff so you need to ask what the role actually entails.

What's it like?

It's a brilliant training ground in dealing with customers. A few months 'working the phones', alongside a good training scheme, will set you up for promotion for all sorts of other jobs. It's undoubtedly hard work. Some call centres have been criticised for being 'the new workhouses', with poor working conditions. Others make the environment and the work as appealing as possible, and many people positively enjoy working there. Certainly, if you like contact with people all day, you may enjoy it.

You'll probably work in a team with individual as well as team sales targets, and if the centre is well managed, you'll enjoy the challenge of working together towards these targets and the bonuses and rewards you get when you reach them.

The day-to-day can sound mundane, but when you're tuning in to new people all day, it doesn't matter that you're not face-to-face with them. You may have a script that appears on-screen once you key in the type of article, or a query the customer makes, and you'll use that to guide you. You'll wear headphones, and take as many calls as possible. This could be between ten or twenty calls an hour, depending on the complexity of the product and the system in use. You'll probably work a shift system, which can be an advantage for people who have family commitments to juggle.

People who do well can move up within the organisation quickly, into supervisory or customer service roles and then perhaps into management.

Skills you need

- A good speaking voice and clear, friendly manner
- Persistence
- An ability to sell, though you will be trained in this
- An ability to learn about the products on offer and relate these to customers' needs
- Confidence
- A quick mind, able to tune into a variety of customers in a short time period and help satisfy their needs.

Getting in and on

Employers advertise in the local press. You can also try Jobcentres (or careers offices if you're straight out of school). If you're interested in local employers you know about, look them up on the Internet or call them. Recruitment officers are pleased to get speculative enquiries for this sort of role, and will give you information and advice.

You won't need specific qualifications but do need to be friendly, polite and have a good speaking voice.

Good employers will train and assess you in NVQ/SVQs. You may be able to sign up for a Modern Apprenticeship or other training scheme (see page 25 for details of these).

(see page 25 for details of these)

CASE STUDY

Carol has worked at a call centre for two years and progressed from a purely sales role to supervisory level. Her company sells a variety of items from catalogues.

'I loved it as soon as I started,' she says. 'I quickly got the hang of it, and the training was good, very intense. They throw you in at the deep end and you either sink or swim – some people only last a few days, but it's just not for some people. You've got to like talking on the phone and getting to know each customer, even for a few minutes. And you've got to be motivated to make the sale – it's no use if you're not interested in reaching targets. The money can be good if you are.

'I was promoted to supervisor after just over a year. I have a team of five plus me, and we sit around a table with a screen and headset each. My job is to motivate and help train the team, especially new team members. I also help with difficult queries, and step in if a customer asks to speak to a manager. When customers phone in they can hear other voices in the background and sometimes they comment on that, and I explain it's because we work like a family. We can't let it get too noisy though. When we're near hitting a target sometimes I have to tone it down.'

Will Carol stay in this sort of work? 'I hope so because it suits me: there's a good atmosphere, I earn well and there are prospects. I feel I'm getting on. I hope to be manager within the next year, running several teams.'

CASHIER OR CHECKOUT OPERATOR

Cashiers work in shops, collecting payment from customers who have already chosen their goods. Many self-service high street and chain stores employ cashiers at a central paying point. Think of electrical out-of-town stores and supermarkets as examples. Department stores also often use cashiers. In other stores the sales staff collect money from the customer as part of one continuous process.

The work

You're based at a till or payment counter, and might scan goods through an electronic system or key prices into the till. It may appear mindless – and some people do work that way – but to do it well you need to be constantly aware of your customer, to be polite and friendly and help with anything that crops up. This could be anything from price-checking to problems with payment. Good cashiers make a difference to how customers view a store, and will encourage them to come back. Good people are also noticed, and you can move on from there to other roles.

Key elements of the job

- You work at a central point within a store
- Customers who have picked up or ordered goods in the store will come to you to pay
- You deal politely and helpfully with customers
- You deal with cash, credit/debit cards, cheques and customer accounts
- You may have to work out change, or the till may tell you how much change to give
- You also tap department codes into the till, so that sales for each department are recorded
- You may weigh fruit and vegetables and help customers pack. You may also get involved in filling shelves, stocktaking or other duties around the store
- You sort out queries and problems that arise
- You need to be aware of security issues, such as what to do if you suspect that a customer is trying to avoid paying for goods
- You might help with ordering, or other associated actions
- You need to keep your work area clean and tidy, and keep track of supplies of bags and adequate amounts of cash in the till
- You may also be in charge of collecting money by post. This could mean checking that all due payments have been received, and sending letters to customers reminding them that their next payment is due.

What's it like?

Handling money is a specialist role, and you'll need training in how the system works. You need to gain the trust of your employers before they'll let you loose on the tills on your own. You'll train off-the-job in an intensive training course, which might last a day or a week, and then start working closely supervised by experienced staff.

You get to see many of the customers who come through the store, but spend less time with them than in a sales role, and may find there is less fulfilment than if you have successfully sold goods to a customer. On the other hand, the diversity of people you are dealing with keeps the job fresh. If you have the right 'people' skills, enjoy dealing with a wide range of customers, and take pride in doing the work well, then it's a good way into retailing if you join a company that's committed to training and moving good staff on.

You may work some sort of shift system including Saturdays and maybe Sundays too. There is often weekend work available while you're still in college, so you can get some experience this way. Remember that part-time temporary staff may not be treated in the same way as full-time permanent employees, so you probably won't have the same degree of ongoing training.

Skills you need

- You need some of the same 'people' skills as sales advisers, but without the specialist sales and product knowledge
- You need to be able to work quickly and accurately
- You need to understand the computer and sales system, and know how to handle money
- You also need to be numerate so that you can understand the figures, give the correct change, and so on
- If the role extends to running credit accounts, you'll learn about banking procedures, printouts and other documents. You won't need this knowledge before you start but numeracy, as above, is important
- You need to be trustworthy and diligent. Tills are counted at the end of each day (sometimes more frequently) and even small discrepancies between the total on the till roll and the amount in the till are a problem.

Getting in and on

Employers recruit through local advertising, Jobcentres and careers services. You can also look online. It'll help to have Maths and English at GCSE, and having more GCSEs is good news, too. But not all employers need you to have these.

Some employers like all their new trainees to spend time on the tills while they start to train them in sales skills and so on. So, if you do well here, promotion can follow. You may be able to gain NVQ/SVQs this way, too.

CASE STUDY

Eric is a university student supplementing his student loan with part-time till-work in a supermarket. 'I work about fifteen hours a week,' he says, 'depending on rotas. Sundays are best as the pay is better but I can't always get that. Evenings are difficult – I'm often tired and have study to do, but the money's not bad.'

What does he like about the role? 'If I'm not too tired I enjoy it. I like the variety of customers, and talking to them. I'm learning a lot about people. I can see how stressed some people are, and how lonely others are. I like this insight into people – I never really mixed outside my own family and friends before.'

Would he take it up as a career? 'I might go for a career in retail management: it's a good place to watch everything that goes on, and I can see the managers in action. I can see it's hard work, though. Being polite to people all the time is very hard work, whether you're on the tills or running the place.'

CUSTOMER SERVICE STAFF

'Customer services' has a wide range of meanings. It can cover any role that takes you into contact with customers, and therefore includes all sales staff and cashiers, as well as those in more specialist roles. Other organisations use it to mean the staff who help customers with queries or problems that aren't dealt with in normal transactions. This is the role outlined below.

The work

There are many incidents that are a bit 'out of the ordinary' in any customer-based operation. Retailing has millions of them! Most are easily resolved if customer service staff are well trained and aware of customer needs. The aim of all customer service work is to satisfy customers so that they will continue to shop at your store. Your work is 'bitty' in one sense, but rewarding in another as you're helping people resolve problems and leave happy.

Key elements of the job

- Different organisations have varying systems for handling customer services
- Many use a counter system where customers can go to a specific place if they have a query. Other staff may work around the till areas or walk around the store helping customers
- You'll ask customers to outline the query, and by speaking with other staff, talking it over with the customer, or using the computer, you'll resolve the problem.
- Most queries are standard and you'll resolve them straight away or within a couple of minutes. This could include faulty goods being brought back for refunds, in which case you'll go through a set procedure and give the customer a refund in cash or onto their credit/debit card
- Queries might be more complex, or need immediate and urgent action. A customer may be injured, for instance, and need first aid. You would call for the first aider to attend, or even call an ambulance
- There might be a child lost in the store, and you'd need to take immediate action to locate the child and calm the parent
- Occasionally, customers can be angry and perhaps obstructive. In this case you will do all you can but may then call in the customer service or department manager
- As a customer services manager you'll handle more complex queries and also report incidents and get involved in policy making. You'll recruit, train and motivate staff, and perhaps plan rotas to allow them to have some time in customer services and stints in other departments
- To do this, you'll build a knowledge of the organisation's sales and customer services policies and ensure that all staff know them.

What's it like?

If you like problem solving and constant contact with people then you'll love it. It's varied, and you never know what's going to happen next. Although there can be difficult moments, good employers will train you to deal with anything that could happen, from shoplifting to a major incident involving evacuating the store. Of course, these incidents don't happen often, but working with the unexpected makes it an interesting role. There is also routine work but if you do well in this role, then the organisation will promote you to use these people-skills in more senior roles.

Skills you need

- You need to be a positive, bubbly 'people' person, and to remain calm in difficult or pressured situations
- This includes always remaining polite, friendly and tactful with difficult and rude customers
- You need to be genuinely interested in people and want to help them
- You also need an ability to focus on the task in hand and not be distracted by a queue or other tasks
- An ability to 'read' a person from their manner and body language, and respond well, is important
- You need to be able to use a computer to enter the details of all queries and their resolutions
- Good communication skills are important
- You must be smart, with a lively mind, and numerate to handle financial transactions
- You need a good general education, and employers will probably want Maths and English at GCSE plus a couple more subjects. But if you can persuade them that you have people-skills and are numerate then GCSEs aren't so important.

Getting in and on

- You can enter as a cashier or sales assistant and work up to customer services, or move into customer services management through a general management scheme
- Some employers ask their good sales staff to spend a part of their time in customer services, so that their roles are varied. Others may ask employees with the right skills and experience to move over to customer services entirely
- Good people may gain promotion into customer services management rapidly. Some spend time in this role before moving into other retailing functions, while others choose to remain in customer services
- You may be able to join a Modern Apprenticeship scheme or another form of training leading to NVQ/SVQs.

Alain works in customer services for a large supermarket chain. He spends part of his time in this department, handling customer queries, and also spends time serving in the bakery, delicatessen and other departments.

'I started stacking shelves and helping customers with general queries, then was asked to serve customers behind one of the counters. From there, I started doing short duties on customer services. I like this though sometimes it's hard to be polite to customers who feel like they're just making a fuss for the sake of it. For instance, we have a scheme to refund the cost of a bottle of wine if a customer doesn't like the wine. There doesn't have to be anything wrong with it. Some customers bring in a nearly empty bottle and say they didn't like it! We still give them their money back but I think it's a cheek. But I'm always friendly and helpful – that's our policy. It's not always easy.'

DISPLAY STAFF

Although we do much of our shopping through necessity, we buy some of our purchases after being tempted by gorgeous window displays or well-thought-out in-store promotions. These are created by display staff.

The work

Display assistants (also known as designers or visual merchandisers) set up window displays creating the best possible show to passers-by. These are themed according to particular promotions, or the time of year, or a certain festival. Setting up a window display isn't as straightforward as it might seem: there can be months of planning and construction involved behind the scenes before the window is actually created. This planning might happen at head office, with the finished design and materials handed down, or in-store display staff might be involved from the start and think the whole project through from the beginning.

Key elements of the job

■ Displays begin with a concept: yours, or given to you by your manager. This could be decided after brainstorming certain themes or seasons. It needs to be eye-catching, attractive, simple enough to stand out yet complex enough to engage the customer. Originality also helps, and although there are only a limited number of ideas, a fresh twist on an old theme is important

- As well as themes and ideas, you need to think practically: what space do you have and how can it be used to best effect? Can you hang items from the ceiling, for instance? If you do, will the wires show?
- After devising, costing and agreeing the concept you need to plan it in detail. This means working out what materials are needed and how everything in the display is going to be obtained, built and delivered
- After producing a detailed plan, and agreeing it with management, it's important to double-check that it fits in with store managers and their ordering and sales plans for that time. There's no point tempting shoppers if there are no stocks of the goods in the store
- Once all the planning's done, triple-checked, ordered and agreed, when the appropriate time comes around you need to be there in that window, dismantling the old display (and returning goods to the appropriate departments) and putting up the new one. This needs to be done professionally and as fast as possible as you're in full view of the public. It used to involve a lot of Sunday work but since Sunday opening, more work is undertaken at night, so as not to distract shoppers during opening hours. Antisocial hours are more likely to be worked by freelance staff and those working in the larger city department stores
- It takes time and energy to create a display: you'll need to obtain the relevant goods from departmental managers who may not always be ready for you or even want you to have the goods that were agreed. These may come from a large number of different departments. You'll have a lot of walking and carrying to do. Then, the window needs to be created perfectly, the pre-made elements have to fit and look pristine, and the additional elements you add, such as the goods and props, need to be perfect. There's a lot of tweaking, standing back and tweaking some more
- Once you've perfected a window, you'll move to the next and the one after that. If you're part of a larger organisation you may move around the region or the whole country, perhaps constructing the same displays in each store. You'll need to amend them to take account of the space available. Often, displays around the country show different stock items, as shoppers make differing choices according to location (fashions and demographics vary around the country: some areas

might have more older people, for instance)
- If you create displays in one store or area then this might be only a part of your job
- You might be responsible for the entire internal design of the store; in larger stores a designer or design team will deal with this.

What's it like?

It's a demanding role, both in terms of finding work (it's a glamorous side of the industry, and many people want to get into it), as well as mentally, artistically and physically. The workload can be gruelling, especially on the road. There are long days of creating and dismantling displays.

It's a creative side of retailing, especially once you've worked your way into more senior roles with autonomy for the store you work in or the windows you dress. It's a chance to create from scratch and make a positive contribution to the store's profitability in a complete project that everyone can see, and that can be very satisfying. Yet there will be days when everything seems to go wrong, and other times when you can't seem to come up with the good ideas. To get around this, some stores use freelance display staff, so that they can bring new minds into the equation when displays feel stale. If you work freelance in this way your reputation is only as good as your last window, so there's pressure to get it right. However, when you do, there's a great buzz.

Skills you need

- You need a range of top creative skills: visual skills, with a flair for colour, shape and overall design. All this alongside a limitless imagination
- You also need to have good communications skills, be adaptable, and work well in a team
- You must be a driven, competitive person who's prepared to work hard, not just at the work itself but at your career
- You need some good GCSEs including English and an art subject. Recruiters are usually looking for people from age 18 onwards, so some A-levels are also useful, though not vital if you work your way up. Some people study for a degree in an art or design subject, or in a

specific course tailored to display careers. See the UCAS database of courses for a full listing of what's available (UCAS details on page 87).

Getting in and on

As a school leaver, you could gain general retail experience and then move across into display work. Good employers will nurture your interest in display and send you on courses, but you'll have to prove yourself first.

The British Display Society offers qualifications run at further education colleges. Courses include work experience in stores, animation studios, prop-making workshops and so on (see their website for details). They will send a pack of information on receipt of a stamped addressed envelope, and are happy to talk with you about education choices if you call them.

You could apply for a graduate training course specifically designed for display work once you have a relevant degree. Before applying for degree courses, look at the recruitment literature of the larger employers and talk to as many as you can, as well as your careers adviser. Try calling recruitment offices and asking about the work and the best way in.

Once you have enough experience you might take a supervisory or management role and design the concepts and 'travelling shows'. There's a range of possibilities with larger employers, though there are limited long-term advancement opportunities. Many display staff work freelance and prefer the variety of this, though organising your own work requires business skills and time spent marketing, collecting payment, etc.

CASE STUDY

Joseph works as a freelance 'window dresser', as the job was known when he started twenty five years ago. He specialises in up-market department stores, which often use freelance designers to give an innovative edge to their window displays. 'I travel all the time,' he says. 'Although most of my work is in London, I have customers spread over a wide area and might only spend a day or two at a location, though often it's longer.'

What does he like about his work? 'I'm a creative person and need to use this in my work: I find that I am continually thinking creatively. That's very important to me. I enjoy the challenge of taking on board new ideas and tailoring them in my own way.'

And what are the downsides? 'The business side, definitely. I'm lucky that my wife handles that for me, as it takes an enormous amount of time. I sometimes miss having colleagues, but I visit my clients continually so do get to know their in-house teams. Getting work is also dependent on the economy – when times are difficult my clients rely more on their own staff for design work.'

HEAD OFFICE ROLES

Every organisation needs a central person or group of people to run it. If it's a small shop, this person might be the owner. He or she would do everything that's needed to keep the business running smoothly. As well as ordering stock and selling it to customers, the owner would:

- rent the premises
- pay the rates and other bills
- recruit staff
- set up and run a computer system, and so on.

When the organisation grows, the owner recruits other people to perform these functions. These functions or roles are sometimes known as head office or central functions in larger organisations. They cover everything that any business needs to do, as well as some specialist retailing functions. Each function may consist of a department of many dozens of people, though some are smaller and more specialist. So you can work in any of the business functions such as finance, IT or human resources and do this within the retailing industry.

Many head office roles involve travelling around the stores to implement policy or gain feedback on what's happening. For more information on the work involved, see careers guides on these particular functions or roles. Also look at the websites of larger retailers.

These are the main functions most large retailers run from head office:

Buying

Large retailers usually buy centrally, their decisions following on from research and policy. Once buying policy is made, then individual buyers work to that brief. See the section on buying (page 32) for more information.

Corporate affairs

This department looks after the image of the organisation. The work includes dealing with press enquiries, writing press releases, organising press conferences, lobbying government and the EU, and generally promoting the retailing industry and your particular organisation within in. You'll need to be an excellent communicator verbally and in writing, outgoing, and able to think on your feet.

You can get into corporate affairs by working your way through from general management or after experience in a specialist agency or an associated area such as PR.

Customer service

This is a store-level activity but policy needs to be made centrally. For instance, what is the policy on returned goods? Data needs to be collected, so that information about problems with certain items can be passed on to buying and other departments. Customer service work in-store, and how to get into it, is discussed on page 41.

Design

This ties in with display work (see page 44). A large retailer wants to display a consistent image throughout all its stores, so its head office design team will work out themes, colourways and even the smallest detail of design in all the stores around the country. They will also order displays to be made and delivered, for installation by travelling display staff. There may be local input into how displays are finished.

Finance

In this department, you manage the business's budgets and financial targets. Individual managers are responsible for reporting their stores' financial results. However, you'll analyse all results, looking for patterns of growth and comparing these with budget, and so on. You need to be numerate with a degree in Finance, Maths or Economics, or something related, to get onto the training scheme of one of the larger retailers. There may be opportunities with smaller local retailers with less specific degrees. You'll still have to demonstrate your numeracy within your degree as well as your motivation, however. Employers will train you over a number of years for one of the professional accountancy qualifications.

Human resources or personnel

Again, this function is carried out at store level as well as centrally. The company's human resources (its staff) are an important asset. Staff need to be carefully chosen, then trained and nurtured. This training is often undertaken by a specialist training department (see below) but the administration, and issues such as salary changes and promotions as well as other support work are handled through human resources (also known as personnel). You need to be patient and have well developed interpersonal skills. You can enter personnel through a specialist training scheme as a graduate, or after gaining experience at store level. It's a function you might move into after starting in sales.

Information Systems (IS) or IT

Retailers need cost-efficient, flexible computer systems to do everything from ordering goods to recording transactions and sending electronic mail. This flow of information is vital – without it, there's no flow of goods. Systems allow buyers to travel less by showing products effectively on-screen, as well as operations to be planned and implemented, demand to be forecast, and so on. Much of the work is with non-IT staff, gleaning or imparting information to allow systems to be developed or used effectively.

Most IT, or IS, trainees enter as graduates, and some recruiters like a relevant degree while others aren't so concerned so long as it has an element of IT within it. Linguists often make good IT analysts, for instance. You need a strong interest in systems and data management as well as getting on well with people at all levels. Training involves working in different departments to learn about all aspects of the business, and also specialist skills training in-house or at college.

Marketing

Marketing staff carry out market research to find out exactly what customers want in terms of their shopping and the products they buy, and then devise marketing campaigns, such as advertising and promotions, to fit this. These campaigns could include anything from prime-time TV ads, to product placement in fashion shoots, to 'two for the price of one' coupons delivered though household doors. In this way new customers are drawn in and old ones kept interested.

Marketing trainees are taken on by the larger employers. You'll need a degree in any subject, as well as a strong interest and preferably some work experience in a marketing-related area. You might enter marketing later after training in general management in stores.

Merchandising

Merchandising is an important role specific to the retailing industry, and is described in detail on page 58.

Other functions

Retailing is a complex business and there are many vital roles that may be represented by only one member of staff or by a small team. Often, these are staffed by specialists trained elsewhere, or staff move sideways and grow into these roles. Other functions include: policy and strategy; trading; scientific and technical (research and development); property services; legal and secretariat; international; logistics; food services; security; warehousing and distribution (this is an area related to retailing rather than strictly a part of it, and is described on pages 74 and 77).

Getting in and on

There are career opportunities in all these areas. With some, you need to be experienced in-store first. An example is customer service: to move into head office here, you might enter retailing through a management training scheme or work your way up as a school leaver and gain the appropriate experience in stores before applying for head office roles.

Other functions, such as finance and IS, recruit directly from universities and may require specific degrees. Here, you'd train in head office and gain a professional qualification. There are also openings for people who have trained in these functions in other industries and want to move into the retailing industry.

You can also find support roles such as administration in head offices, and this can be a way into specialist areas, too.

There are openings at board level (the top rung of management) in many of these areas.

CASE STUDY

Head office work: marketing officer

Jennifer works for a chain of electrical stores as marketing officer at their head office. She graduated with a degree in Geography and joined the management training scheme two years ago. After spells in various departments she settled into the marketing department, and has been there for nine months. 'I love marketing,' she says. 'It's a dynamic and exciting place to work. Everyone is very creative and we work as a team to pull together effective campaigns.' Her role is to market the company's goods, which means devising ways of promoting and increasing sales though strategies such as advertising. 'I wasn't sure about marketing before I joined the department: I had an idea I might remain in branch and go into store management, but this is definitely what I want to do.'

Part of her role involves understanding the customer and what the customer wants: 'We do a lot of market research, commissioning specialist agencies to find out exactly who our customers are and what they think. It's vital that we have this information as we can't hope to reach customers successfully without it.'

Does she miss working in a branch? 'In some ways, but I visit branches as part of my work, and I'm in touch with what's going on. Some of the work concerns localised marketing campaigns and these involve more branch contact. I like being part of a specialist team like this but with colleagues throughout the UK. This job is like being in marketing and also in retail: I could move sideways into a marketing role outside retail but I'm developing specialist skills here all the time and these apply specifically to the retail industry. I love the whole buzz of retail anyway: I wouldn't want to leave it.'

MANAGER

The term 'management' can mean different things. You can be a personnel manager, an IT manager or a financial manager within the retail industry, and each of these roles is quite different. But the term 'retail management' (or retail sales management, or in-store retail management) means running a store or cluster of stores, and this section describes that role. There are notes at the end about other types of management within retailing.

The work

Retail sales managers run stores. They are responsible for every aspect of the store (or stores) they are in charge of, and ultimately responsible for their store's profitability. Some managers have great autonomy over buying, recruiting, and so on. Others, and this is more usual, have strong direction and input from head office in many areas of running the store. Larger organisations are more centrally run. It's the manager's responsibility to put together

- the elements handed down from head office
- along with individual ideas and methods

in a way that delivers a profitable, buzzing store full of buying customers served by happy staff.

Managers of all but the smallest stores have assistant or departmental managers working for them, who report regularly (daily, or more frequently) to the manager with details of sales levels, any problems in supply, staffing and so on.

Key elements of the job

- Your overall aim is to improve the performance of the company: this means delivering the best possible profits from your store, meeting central targets, and keeping a close eye on everything that happens in your store

- You are involved in as much customer contact and selling as is possible: you never simply hide away in an office reviewing figures and writing reports
- You motivate and lead the store's staff to ensure that everything within the store runs efficiently and that customers receive the highest level of service, whoever they come across in-store
- You deal with people ranging from customers to the highest-level executives of the organisation
- You handle all areas of the store's operations at these different levels – you might discuss profit with a financial assistant, design issues with the design director and the quality of produce with an elderly customer
- You handle the problems that more junior staff cannot resolve, including the more difficult customer queries and complaints
- You're responsible for security, locking up at the end of the day, for instance, as well as health and safety
- You feed information back to head office, partly through the electronic systems installed in tills and for stock taking, and also through reporting customer reactions to goods and designs, and so on. Reviewing this information, you might take direct action to improve the store, or decisions might be made centrally
- You keep an eye on what's happening with competing stores: their prices, products, systems, any innovations, anything that changes
- If you manage a smaller store you might also handle supplier accounts and more of the day-to-day paperwork
- The job does vary considerably depending on the size of the organisation, the products you sell and the size and number of stores you manage. You could be primarily involved with daily processes in the store, or more involved with reporting while also motivating your departmental managers.

What's it like?

It's a highly responsible job where you need to keep a clear, objective head as to your priorities while also handling day-to-day details and dealing constantly with a wide range of people. Above all, you need to keep staff motivated, and to do this you need to have a strong 'presence' and ensure that your staff believe in your leadership. This is clearly a demanding role, requiring many skills and great maturity.

It's physically as well as intellectually and emotionally demanding: the hours can be long, especially around times such as Christmas or the sales. You cannot work short hours and expect your staff to work longer hours, so you need to be there setting an example. It involves your presence in the store as much as is possible, so it's physically gruelling, walking the departments, talking with staff and customers, praising good work and offering constructive comments where changes need to be made. In addition to this, you need to travel to head office and around the region, and fit all this into your busy schedule. So you need to develop strong leadership over your assistant managers, who run their departments and are in charge during your absence.

No day ever turns out quite as you expect it to, it's a varied role, and very rewarding for the right person. Spending time in-store on work experience or in early training days will give you an idea of whether it's for you.

Skills you need

You need to be:

- able to deal with a large range of different people. This includes managing and motivating your staff to meet sales targets, so effective leadership skills are important. You also need to be happy to work at any level within your team as needs dictate
- intelligent, good at planning and organising, forward- and quick-thinking, adaptable, and responsive to difficult or unexpected events. This means being able to remain objective when dealing with both macro- and micro-level events and being able to prioritise
- well-presented, polite, tactful, and able and willing to take responsibility early in your career
- mobile, so that your employer can move you between stores within the region and often around the country
- open to new opportunities and possibilities, with the creativity that entails
- interested in all elements of business, whether it's marketing, selling

and negotiating, accounting or reporting orally and on paper. You need to be numerate and IT literate.

Getting in and on

You'll start your management career as either a sales assistant or as a trainee manager in a specific training scheme.

Look under 'sales staff' for entry requirements as a sales assistant (page 65). From working as a sales assistant you'll be pulled into a management development scheme after proving yourself.

To enter directly into a management training scheme you usually need a degree (or equivalent). This can be in any subject. There are also vocational degree/HND courses you can take, often with retailing as a subsidiary subject of a business degree – see the UCAS website for listings of degrees (find the UCAS URL in Further Information on page 87). Some employers accept school leavers with A-levels or equivalent. If you know you want to enter retailing from early on, it's worth looking at vocational qualifications you can take alongside or instead of A-levels while still at school. Speak to your careers adviser as the field of vocational and sixth form qualifications is changing rapidly at the moment.

Recruiters are looking for motivated people who possess the skills and attributes listed above. Some also ask for specifics such as another language or technical ability for specialist retailing. You'll need GCSEs in Maths and English and may have to pass aptitude and skills tests as part of selection for these schemes, which can be very competitive to get onto. You'll progress at your own pace, and high-flyers may find themselves in junior management positions within a year. A more usual timescale is eighteen months to two years, but the pace does appear to be accelerating.

There's more on management training schemes in the section 'Training' on page 26.

Prospects

There are increasing job and career prospects in retailing, and roles are becoming more complex as the industry modernises. Because of this, employers are looking for better qualifications from their trainees and higher achievement once training. If you're good, you can progress extremely fast, through junior management of a small store after a year, perhaps, to running a group of stores and then a region. You may choose to specialise into another type of work within retailing, either from general management or by entering specifically to train in that function. Your work may keep you in-store, or you might be based in head office, or at home if your work involves travelling that region.

The larger the organisation, the more likely there are to be early openings for progression.

Other types of management

Department manager

You'll lead and motivate your staff while also taking a major part in sales and customer service. You'll be responsible for the cleanliness, safety, stock levels, and image of your department, and for meeting efficiency and customer service targets. In some organisations you'll be responsible for, or have some part in, buying decisions too.

Area manager

Here, you'll have responsibility for perhaps ten to twenty stores, motivating and leading the teams from a distance and acting as the link between head office and store level. You have greater authority, and there's more emphasis on strategy. You'll travel more, too, between your stores, visiting each as often as possible to meet the team, motivate, communicate and help with any problems. You could be promoted to regional manager, responsible for two or three areas and more involved at head office and at strategic level.

Managers of specific functions

All the functions described in the section 'Head office roles' (see page 48) offer management opportunities. You can find out more about this work through careers guides specific to those functions.

CASE STUDY

David is general store manager of a large out-of-town supermarket. He started work fifteen years ago after leaving school with A-levels, and has worked in a variety of roles, first as a trainee on the company's management scheme and later as manager of various departments and clusters of departments at a number of stores in the region. He moved to this store as manager a year ago.

'As manager my primary consideration is profitability. The store is successful if it reaches and exceeds its targets, and although I have many roles within the store, this is my primary aim. I have a series of secondary aims, devised to help us reach our goals in terms of profit and also in the elements that contribute to profits. Simply put, these are income and expenditure: we need to maximise our takings whilst keeping our costs at a minimum level without affecting the quality of the goods or service we provide.

'I have a number of key managers working with me towards these aims. For instance, the personnel manager works with me to ensure that we have the right, correctly trained and highly motivated staff on board, that their rotas are working and that wage costs are reasonable. I work with managers of the various departments to ensure that the goods delivered are displayed, sold, marked down as necessary and then moved on if unsold. Wastage is a huge cost if this process if badly managed.

'On a day-to-day level my time is spent either in my office, analysing figures collated from the store or sent from head office, meeting with key personnel, reviewing all elements of the business, and so on. I keep my office time to a minimum as it's vital that I talk with customers and staff as much as possible, and I aim to spend at least fifty per cent of my time on the sales floor, again with key personnel.

'Attention to detail is vital and it can be difficult, sometimes, to 'see' your department clearly if you are working there all day: I help that process by looking, talking and reviewing on an ongoing basis. It's also vital that I am seen to be available and leading the business: staff and customers need a figure they can look up to and turn to, so leadership skills are very important.'

MERCHANDISER

Merchandisers work closely alongside buyers (see page 32) in medium and large organisations, the division of duties between these two roles varying with different organisations. As retailing becomes more complex, merchandising is becoming an increasingly important role.

The work

Very broadly, merchandisers forecast product sales so that the right quantities of the right goods can be ordered and placed in the right stores. They also monitor all elements of product sales, set budgets for buyers, and are responsible for the profits of departments. They may have a range of other responsibilities (see below).

Key elements of the job

This role overlaps with buyers' and display staff's roles, and responsibilities vary from company to company. The role outlined below is a mix of the many responsibilities that merchandisers sometimes have. For more details of specific jobs and training you need to talk directly with employers.

- You'll set budgets for buyers and work closely alongside them
- You'll be responsible for the profits of your departments: forecasting future sales and profits based on analysing figures from past sales and talking with sales staff, and so on. You make your budgets according to the data you collect. Your aim is to ensure that stores are always well-stocked (though not over-stocked) with the right goods for customer demand, and that this is always met. You also need to ensure that you mix high-risk with lower-risk ranges, rather than gambling the whole budget on goods that might not sell. All this time, your aim is to maximise profit
- You'll probably make the final decisions on product design and packaging, either by talking direct with suppliers or through buyers
- You might design or organise in-store displays, working out how best to present the goods, how to ticket them and so on. In smaller stores and organisations, this could be your main responsibility, rather than any forecasting or analysis. Where these displays show goods from one manufacturer, they are known as concessions. You might organise and run concessions in a number of stores
- Your job might involve organising tastings of groceries such as a new biscuit line, or a new soft drink, as an employee of the retailer or the manufacturer
- As you make decisions based on your forecasts you need to be on-hand in the stores, watching sales and speaking with managers and

staff about what's selling. Lines that were over-bought will need to be reduced in price when it comes to sale time, and you need to know this as early as possible as other buying decisions are constantly needing to be made.

What's it like?

This is difficult to sum up as the role varies so much – in some organisations it's a fairly junior post, based around individual promotions or getting the stock looking right in the store. In others it's an analytical and risk-taking role interwoven with that of the whole buying team.

When it's a role giving responsibility for profitability then there'll always be pressure to perform as you're judged on your performance. It's fast-moving as well as pressured. You need to look ahead as well as back, and to keep control of many elements at once. As such, it's complex and demanding. It's also exciting and at the forefront of innovations in retailing. Stores are only as good as their merchandisers and a lot rests of your performance. Because of this, if you prove yourself you'll go places fast.

If you're involved in store promotions it can be intensive in other ways: you might travel from store to store, setting up 'stalls' offering samples or tasters to customers. There's a lot of customer contact, as well as liaising with in-store staff.

Skills you need

- commercial flair, with a head for business and profit, a head for figures, and an interest and ability in analysing these and forecasting trends
- to be creative and forward-thinking, ready to take risks, understand those risks and spread them adequately
- to be interested in innovation with a flair for understanding new concepts and translating those to what will sell
- to get on with all sorts of people, from customers through to the highest level of management. You also need to be able to communicate complex ideas

- energy, and to be able to work fast and hard to deadlines
- to be mobile, moving from store to store and relocating as appropriate. You may also travel overseas to meet suppliers, though this may rest with the buying team.

Getting in and on

You might enter merchandising by working your way up from sales assistant and showing your interest, commitment and ability. You'll then be placed in a merchandising team and learn the role as an assistant merchandiser. You could also be moved into a formal management training or development scheme.

As a graduate (or possibly with A-levels) you could enter a management training scheme direct and either train in a general management role then move sideways into merchandising, or go straight in as a trainee merchandiser. You could start in buying or distribution, which are both closely allied with merchandising.

It's a competitive area, but retailers depend on top merchandisers for their profits and encourage and train the brightest and most able people in this role. If you do well there's a possibility of rapid promotion to a responsible position as merchandiser within a few years of entering retailing.

CASE STUDY

Mandy is a merchandiser for a small fashion chain: 'I trained with one of the large retailers and worked in buying then merchandising, but got fed up with the size of the organisation. I had my own ideas on how the business should be run and the direction our image should be taking. I disagreed with management and a contact offered me work here. It's better because I am autonomous. I make some of the buying decisions too, so I can influence the direction of the company. But I also get to use my analytical skills, and get a kick when my hunches pay off. The company's grown significantly since I joined and part of that is down to my work. That's exciting.'

PERSONAL SHOPPER

Personal shoppers are increasingly important in retail organisations which seek high-spending customers. These customers are limited for time and need help making their purchasing decisions, or they might have the time but are more likely to spend when they have personal attention.

The work

Most large stores now employ personal shoppers. They offer this as a free service to clients, usually in their fashion departments but increasingly over other areas of the store. Customers like the service for two main reasons: firstly, they can use the skills of an experienced and knowledgeable person to advise them, and secondly, as people have less and less time available for shopping, it saves them time.

Key elements of the job

The essence of the work is supplying customers with a high level of expert, personalised service. As a personal shopper you'll perform some or all of these tasks:

- You preselect items in-store for existing customers who have contacted you to make an appointment and who might request a selection of outfits, e.g. for a forthcoming event
- When the customer arrives you spend time together and advise the customer on colour, style, fit and suitability. You may then look for accessories or for a different type of item if those chosen aren't quite right
- Customers may come around the store with you, telling you when they see something they like. You lead them to the most likely items as you get a feel for their taste and the reason for the purchases
- You'll know a customer's budget, and supply items to fit within that budget
- Using your own experience and knowledge of the items in-store, as well as your fashion sense and person-to-person skills, you find the right items and then persuade the customer to buy. Doing this, you build a relationship with the customer, who will return again and

again. You might end up planning the customer's entire wardrobe for them, remembering what is already there and adding to it as required

- You might be asked to supply everything the customer needs from the store, for example you are given a list of events and birthdays, and need to select likely gifts for the customer to choose from
- You might take these items to the customer's home or office, and display them there for their choice. These could all be from one store and you'd be employed by that store. But independent organisations supplying this service are becoming more common and will select items from a number of different stores, as well as procuring theatre tickets and so on
- You take notes as you go, recording purchases and later feedback from clients. In this way you get to know a client's needs and so provide a top service. You also research trends – high fashions, trends in business apparel, and so on, so that you know exactly what to recommend to whom
- You can also set up as a freelance personal shopper, though clearly you'll need plenty of experience and contacts before you get any work
- Some personal shoppers work on commission and earn a percentage of the price of items sold. Others are paid salaries by their employers. Salaried personal shoppers still need to make sales: your sales record will be scrutinised and you'll need to show that you increased turnover for that store through your work.

What's it like?

If you love shopping, this could be a perfect way to work. You get to know a store's stock inside-out and to think about how it will all fit together for particular clients. It's a Barbie-doll dresser's dream come true! However, you are there to serve a client and to satisfy their needs to their particular taste, so it can be frustrating. You might think a certain item is perfect but perhaps it's not what the client is after, or perhaps it's outside the client's budget. Or you may simply not get on with the client, but as a professional you need to get over that and offer the best possible service.

It's also hard work, as you are on your feet most of the day and in constant customer contact. You need to keep abreast of current and future fashions, fabrics, and trends in all sorts of areas such as home technology and travel. Your own personal grooming and fashion sense must be excellent, and this in itself is hard work and expensive.

Skills you need

Apart from liking shopping:

- You must be a good communicator and be able to tune into your customer's mind-frame as well as explain how you envisage items coming together. You also need to be tactful, patient, be able to build relationships and trust
- You need a sense of taste and current trends, and how to mix and match traditionally or eclectically, according to what is required
- You need to be customer-oriented, and always strive to offer the best possible customer service – this is the ultimate in customer service roles
- You need to understand fashion, clothes, fabrics, colour and shape, or the equivalent if you are working in a different department. You need to show customers that you understand this by the way you dress, groom yourself and talk about the items
- You'll need to get to know the products within the store and have a strong interest in all of the relevant items so that you can bring them to mind in discussion or planning.

Getting in and on

This is a job you get into after other retail experience: no store is going to let you loose on their best customers until you have proved yourself in the ways described above, and got to know the store's products. Starting in sales is a good way in, demonstrating your skills while showing an interest in this role as you progress. It will take a number of years as customers need to sense a solid grounding in customer service and product knowledge. It's also an area some merchandisers move into. Wherever you start, it's seen as a 'plum job' and you'll have to show you are a top salesperson and very committed.

You might choose to go freelance as a personal shopper, attracting your own clients and being paid an hourly rate. You will need an excellent client base, however. You need a full contacts book and to be sure of yourself and the market. Some freelance personal shoppers start in-store in a salaried role and develop their client base that way. Another possibility is working for a company that offers shopping services: look in your Yellow Pages for local companies, or on the Internet.

SALES STAFF

As retailing is about selling goods or services to customers, the sales role is crucial. There are many essential back-up roles within the retailing industry but sales is the role they all underpin.

The work

Your job is to help customers buy. There are plenty of different job titles for people in retail sales – sales assistant, sales adviser, customer services assistant (though this has another meaning, see the section on page 41), partner, colleague . . . Whatever you're called, you are the public face of your organisation and your job is to welcome, help, and sell as much as reasonably possible to each customer. In practice, this usually means a 'soft sell' rather than hammering your customer with aggressive sales talk. In effect, it means that whenever you have customer contact (which can be constantly, or it can be mixed in with other duties) you do your best to help the customer, and encourage them to buy the right goods for their needs.

Sales is essential training for any career within retailing (and invaluable in other work and life situations) and you need to ensure you have some sales experience whatever you want to end up doing.

Key elements of the job

■ Most sales roles involve contact with customers most of the time, though your job may also involve stocking shelves, tidying and so on. Smaller shops tend to give more variety to the work as there is less staff around to specialise

- Some sales work is done via the telephone, but the principle of the role is the same whether you're on the phone or face-to-face
- Some sales roles involve simply taking payment at the till. In this case, other staff will be available within the store to advise customers and replenish stocks on the shelves, etc. Most organisations swap you around from one role to another through the day and week. If you do well at these roles you should be promoted to roles involving more customer contact, and perhaps more selling skills (encouraging the customer to buy) rather than simply taking payment
- Sales roles in other organisations involve an entire sales 'pitch' from when the customer first enters the store (or calls on the telephone). First of all, you welcome your customer. As you do this, you assess their needs and start to interest them in goods you think they might want. You offer help and advice about the goods on offer. When you feel they are satisfied with what you are offering, you 'close' the sale (ask the customer to agree to buy it), take payment and arrange delivery. You may also provide after-sale support to your customer
- You need to be aware of security procedures, as well as health and safety (so that you'd know what to do if a customer tried to steal an item, and how to empty the store in an emergency situation)
- You may use computer systems for stock control and ordering. This is automatic at computerised checkouts where bar codes input data on items being bought and lead into automatic ordering. You may have other input into this system, too
- Cleaning up and keeping displays tidy and full may be part of your job. You may also talk to customers who are bringing back faulty goods, and arrange refunds.
- You may become a specialist sales assistant or adviser, especially in larger stores or if you're selling technical goods where customers need responses to technical queries: if the sales assistant is knowledgeable about all technical aspects, the customer has more confidence to buy
- Salespeople need some knowledge and understanding of the product range as well as the competitors' ranges (goods sold by other organisations). In some roles this knowledge can be minimal; in other roles it needs to be thorough
- In all roles, customers expect good service, whether it's a fast whiz though the checkouts or detailed and helpful information on goods. A

salesperson's role is always to give this service efficiently and courteously.

What's it like?

Some stores, such as supermarkets, are organised to give fast, efficient shopping with minimal staff contact. Others, such as department stores, rely on personal service to each customer. Obviously, working in such different places will give a different type of experience.

Your experience also depends on who you work for. In a small shop this will be the manager, and you might have to 'act up' as manager during breaks or busy times, even when you have little experience. There might be less formal training but more on-the-spot experience. In larger stores you'll work for a supervisor, department manager then manager, so you'll have a more gradual introduction to the other processes going on around you.

Wherever you work, it's hard work physically – expect to be completely exhausted to begin with. Adjusting to different customers and their differing needs all the time is also demanding. It can be monotonous at quieter times, which is why many organisations swap their staff from tills to shop floor to filling shelves, to give a break and some variety. But if you enjoy being around people and helping customers get the best experience then you'll like the interaction.

It's worth finding the right type of organisation for you: spend some time 'shopping' in various types of stores, and watch and listen. Would you enjoy this work? Which types of store and types of product interest you most? This is a career where you can go and spectate before you start, so make the most of that opportunity. It's also easy to get weekend or holiday work. Remember that your experience as a school or college student working part-time will be different from people on training schemes who are working towards targets and learning as they go.

Skills you need

These roles suit people with the right personality rather than specific educational qualifications, so they are a great way into a career if you don't have much to show on paper. Equally, people with good qualifications need to start their retailing career here. Whatever your background, you need to:

- have loads of common sense
- be reasonably numerate – understanding numbers and being able to work out change and whether a transaction is right
- have the ability to talk easily with all sorts of people, as well as listen
- be able to learn about the customer, products, organisation and sales techniques
- be able to follow standard procedures and also to respond to unexpected events
- be interested in negotiating, explaining things, and providing information
- be able to work well when it's busy as well as when it's quiet
- not be upset by difficult customers, remaining polite and not taking things personally
- be tactful and helpful
- have a good memory for remembering customers and tasks that you may have to delay carrying out when under pressure
- be patient and calm, even under pressure
- work in a team
- have loads of stamina for long hours standing or sitting
- always be well presented, wearing either the uniform provided or your own clothes as appropriate for the job
- be able to cope with more mundane tasks such as filling shelves and cleaning up
- overall, to genuinely like people and be pleased to be dealing with them all day.

Getting in and on

Anyone over 16 can go into retail sales. Some companies ask for more educational qualifications than others, but when it comes to it, it's your personality that matters. If you don't have the required passes at GCSE it's still worth talking to recruiters.

Larger recruiters usually ask for at least Maths and English grades C or above at GCSE. Some ask for more than this. Others set basic tests at interview to check on English and Maths. As well as this, you'll need to talk easily at interview and show an interest in the organisation, the goods and retailing as a career.

Look for work through your careers office, local press advertisements, or phone around companies that interest you and ask to speak to someone in their personnel or human resources department. They'll be happy to let you know what openings there are and to send you more information. Ask in particular for training schemes such as Modern Apprenticeships. These can fill up sooner than you might expect so find out and apply as early as possible. Your careers adviser or your local Learning and Skills Council can give you more information about these schemes and local employers running them. See Further Information for more details (page 84).

Most training is on-the-job, working with someone more experienced. This should be supplemented by off-the-job sessions. Large organisations may send you for days or weeks of training at centres in other locations. Your initial training may take many weeks of short courses and supervised work in various departments and areas of the organisation.

Prospects

Retailing is a fast-moving industry and if you're a quick learner you'll progress rapidly with the right organisation. Everyone who works in retailing needs sales experience – it's never wasted time. You may choose to remain on the shop floor dealing with customers then work your way up to supervisor, department manager and store manager. From there you might become area or regional manager, and there are more opportunities further up the ladder still.

Others prefer to move sideways into other functions such as display work, buying, or some of the head office roles. Again, if you're keen and show aptitude for the work, employers will make the most of your skills.

Over half the people working in the industry are part-time and there are options open if you want to do this, though much of the part-time work is at lower levels. With good employers you'll be able to progress as a part-timer, though more slowly.

Good employers will also encourage you to work towards NVQ/SVQs, either as part of a Modern Apprenticeship or outside this scheme. See the section on training, page 23.

Smaller stores may not have the same breadth or depth of training schemes available, though you'll probably gain greater responsibility early on if you're good. You may not be able to become manager if the manager owns the store, but as you gain experience you should become a more senior sales assistant and your pay should reflect this.

CASE STUDY

Ellie has worked as a sales assistant in a high street fashion store for one year, since leaving school with three GCSEs. 'I always wanted to work in fashion,' she says, 'and this is the best place to start. I always loved shopping and dressing up. Now I help other people do it.'

Her job includes stocking the rails, ticketing, marking goods down for the sales, and cleaning up after customers. She also spends time as a changing room assistant. 'You have to be careful – you never know who's going to try to steal something. I count items in and out but as well as that, I talk to customers and help them if they want help. It's a way of making it harder to steal things, as well as helping genuine customers.' Her main role is in the store, helping customers with queries and taking payment at the till. 'I thought the system was complicated when I started but it seems easy now. Sometimes things go wrong but there's always a supervisor to help.' Ellie hopes to be promoted to supervisor herself, soon.

She works a rota which gives her one complete weekend off in three. Other weekends she works Saturdays and sometimes Sundays.

'When it's quiet it can get boring,' she says, 'but when it's busy it's fun. I'm learning a lot. I'm starting an NVQ soon too, so that I'll get qualifications. I'd like to get on, and be manager or even area manager one day.'

SELF-EMPLOYED TRADER

Rather than working for a retailing company or shopkeeper, you can set up your own retail business. To start with this will probably be as a sole trader, perhaps on a market stall, where your overheads (costs) are relatively low. Later, you might buy the lease of a shop, develop your business into a company employing other people, and so on. Some people set up shops because they have always wanted to run their own business and this is the best way to do it at the time. Others come at it from a retailing angle – they love retail and want to do it for themselves. Whichever way, the principles are the same.

The work

Working for yourself is tough: there is no one to motivate you and no one to pay your wages in bad months. The up-side can be tremendous: being your own boss, developing a brilliant idea through to a profit-making business, challenging the world and winning. It's not something to go into without plenty of experience, advice and training though, as detailed below.

Key elements of the job

- You find a retail idea that you believe is going to work, and develop it from there. This might be a new product or series of products that you believe will sell, or you might see that there is a gap in the market for shoe shops in your town, for instance, or you might think you can sell goods cheaper than your competitors and still make a profit. There are many possibilities
- You research this idea thoroughly and once you're sure of it, have taken as much advice and gone on as many training days as possible, you research it all over again
- You might find someone to back you financially (friend, family, or bank), and perhaps people to come into the business as partners or employees
- You set up your business, probably in a small way as you won't have the money to spend on a large shop and all the fittings: and anyway, how much do you want to risk?
- You trade, hopefully make a profit (or at least, not too large a loss) in the first year or two, and expand from there
- Perhaps one day you sell your chain of shops to one of the large organisations, who may keep your trading name and brand while incorporating the chain into their operations. You then retire to the sun. Or, more likely if you're an entrepreneur, start up all over again.

What's it like?

Working for yourself is hard. When you have a job you are looked after by your employer: you are trained, assessed, paid, nurtured and (hopefully) made to feel good about the work you do. Working for yourself, you probably have none of this: it's just you plus your business idea, plus a lot of hard work ahead. The work never ends, because the shop needs to be open all day and you need to redecorate that damp patch on the wall in the evenings. After that you need to do the daily paperwork and then the monthly books and accounts, then think about reordering stock . . . somewhere, you need to fit in eating and sleeping.

Many businesses end in failure, often leaving their owners with debts. Entrepreneurs (people who set up businesses) are usually very motivated people who have the drive to overcome the hard work and problems that arise, and to see clearly though the daily nitty gritty. You need to know that it's not only what you want to do as a career, but also how you want to live your life.

Skills you need

You need knowledge: about the retail industry, the lines you hope to set up in, how to run a business, and a multitude of other aspects. Experience of retailing is essential. In addition, you need to be an all-rounder, able to deal with an angry customer as well as keep the financial records and negotiate good deals from your suppliers. This list gives you some idea of the range of skills required:

- Sales skills: understanding how people tick; communicating with them; closing the sale
- Management skills: leadership; planning; decision-making; personal and general responsibility
- Administrative skills: prioritising; organising; book-keeping; knowing the legalities
- Looking ahead: continuing to learn; open-mindedness
- Ideas and pizzazz: finding new opportunities and ideas; problem-solving; original thinking; lateral thinking; objectivity; ambition; risk-taking
- Hard-working: working long hours; doing every job yourself; flexibility.

There are more: this list is abridged from *Getting into Self-employment* by Joanna Grigg (published by Trotman). Find this or another book on self-employment for an overview of what it entails and the knowledge and skills you need.

Getting in and on

You may take over someone else's retail business, join someone as their partner or set up from scratch on your own or with partners. Whatever you're planning, you need to get good business advice. Never sign anything until you are sure that you are ready to make the business commitment. Get legal advice each time before signing. Go to your local Enterprise Agency (free, in each large town and city – look under the name of your town or ask at your careers centre or Jobcentre).

CASE STUDY

Shahed runs his own takeaway food business in a seaside resort. He set it up three years ago when the lease on another takeaway became available: 'I saw that there was potential for a curry takeaway on that site,' he says. 'Although there are plenty in the town, there were none in this area and none offering what I offer: real home cooking, and good vegetarian food. Some of my friends told me that they eat less meat than they used to, and I could see that we were selling more vegetarian dishes at the restaurant where I worked, so I thought the market would be there.'

He researched the business thoroughly. 'I asked around my own community to see whether people would buy my food. There wasn't a great deal of enthusiasm, I have to admit, because we are a close-knit community and most families cook wonderful food at home already. There was some interest, though. My father was behind the idea, and didn't mind me leaving the family business. So then I asked people who weren't part of the community: fellow students from my HNC course, for instance, and they asked around for me. I also stopped people in the street – I had a clipboard and a few simple questions. I got a lot of impartial feedback that way.'

Shahed got ideas for his market research from his local Enterprise Agency. 'They stressed the fact that there has to be a market before you try to sell into it: although I knew that intuitively because my family have always been in business, it helped to have it spelled out. I did as much market research as I could before I bought the lease.'

He kept his outgoings as low as possible, and financed the first year through his family. Family and community members helped by working for low wages to get him started. 'It's going well,' he says, 'though it was slow to start with and I used to worry about it all the time. I work very hard, but I like being in charge. I love it when people ask me what to do and I know the answers – that's a great buzz.'

WAREHOUSE STAFF

Warehouses are storage areas away from the store (those attached to the store are smaller, and called stock rooms) where goods are taken between production and the store. Clearly, the less stock (goods) a retailer has in a warehouse, the better, as it is taking up space, and is money doing nothing. Some retailers own their own warehouses while others use a warehousing company to store and transport their ordered goods.

Some stores operate without stock rooms so they can use all the space for selling. But most have these areas for unloading, unpacking, sorting and storing goods arriving from the warehouse.

The work

Warehousing and distribution go together: a warehouse is simply a stop-off point in the distribution process. So if you work in warehousing, much of the work is to do with transportation. Goods are received from manufacturers in large quantities, usually according to retailers' orders. In the warehouse you receive them, break them down into smaller units as required, and store them. You ensure that storage conditions are correct: some goods must be kept chilled, for instance, while others must be kept upright.

When a retailer needs the goods, an order comes through and items are picked from the shelves, packed into loads for transport and sent off. This sounds simple but one warehouse might deal with many hundreds of destinations, lines of goods and retailers. Getting it right is essential, and you need to understand complex systems to make it work efficiently.

Key elements of the job

There are many different jobs within warehousing: fork-lift drivers, pickers, assemblers, porters, and trailer drivers do the main warehousing and distribution work. Leading them are warehouse and transport supervisors and managers. As well as these roles there are specialist systems roles, designing and updating the complex computer systems that control the warehouse, as well as data-input staff and a whole range of support roles.

Because of this there's no one 'job' to describe. All the people involved work as a team, and are skilled at their work. Many of the drivers within warehouses need specialist driving qualifications by law. Others are experienced and qualified in other ways. They work towards making the most efficient use of the space available. This is becoming more and more important as retailers keep less and less stock on-site, and require 'just-in-time' delivery. Orders must be received, items located and picked, then adequately packed and sent off. Managers must know exactly how long this process will take. Computers help, down to the last detail, such as telling the fork-lift drivers which items to pick first from the shelves to allow easier despatch and packing or more efficient delivery.

What's it like?

Warehouses are large places full of machinery, often noisy or cold. Some are run by computer to such an extent that fork-lift trucks are guided electronically, and there may be few people out on the warehouse floor. So the environment can vary considerably, with much of the work being done either in offices or in the warehouse and at despatch. It can be hard work physically and mentally, requiring long periods of concentration in an area where one mistake could be costly or dangerous.

Skills you need

- You must be fit for many of the jobs on offer, with plenty of stamina
- Health and safety are prime considerations in this environment so you need to understand the importance of, and stick to, regulations
- Other roles require specialist skills, such as in IT and management. See other sections for details here.

Getting in and on

As with mainstream retailing careers you can enter warehousing straight after taking GCSEs and without any formal qualifications, though the more you have the better. You may need to have Maths and English at GCSE. Your training options may be limited until you reach 18 as this is the age for learning to drive some of the specialist machinery.

Modern Apprenticeships can be taken, as for mainstream retailing, in Distribution and Warehousing – see page 25 for more information.

Larger recruiters run management training schemes, taking people with A-levels and degrees. These schemes are generally geared up for people with some retail, management or warehousing experience.

RELATED AREA: WHOLESALING AND DISTRIBUTION

Wholesaling is a separate function from retailing and as such, has its own structure, complexities and careers. This brief section aims to summarise wholesaling as a function rather than a career. This is to help you understand this related process whilst you are researching your retailing career.

What is wholesaling?

Retailing, as this book explains, entails selling goods to the end consumer. This consumer is the individual customer in the shop (or via email and post) who needs the goods. Wholesaling, like retailing, also involves the supply chain (see page 8) but doesn't supply the end consumer. Instead, the goods travelling down the chain stop at another business. An example is builders' merchants. These are specialist wholesalers which supply the building industry. If you are a builder and need several tonnes of builder's sand, you can order this from the builders' merchant, but if you own your own home and need a plank of wood, they can't help you. They deal in large quantities and provide a different type of sales service, often assuming specialist knowledge of their customers.

Many large wholesalers employ their own specialists working in the head office roles as well as design, buying, production, warehousing and distribution. They have their own career structures similar to those within retailing but clearly not focussing on the individual customer. But sales is still an important aspect of the work, and business-to-business sales such as those involved in wholesaling involve high-level skills and their own career paths.

Smaller wholesalers, like smaller retailers, offer more limited career paths, but working for a smaller organisation will give you a broader view of the functions within it.

One common type of wholesaler is the cash and carry wholesaler. These organisations sell goods to independent retailers. The retailers then divide the larger quantities down to individual, saleable units and use them to stock their stores. Cash and carry wholesalers, as their name implies, do not use distributors but their customers collect goods from their depots themselves.

Distribution

Just as successful warehousing (which is a part of retailing – see page 8) is dependent on efficient distribution systems, so too is successful wholesaling. There are specialist career paths entirely within distribution (which may involve both wholesaling and retailing). Specialists analyse the existing distribution networks and devise new networks and systems with increased efficiency. Wholesalers and retailers might employ their own distribution experts or might contract this work out to specialist distribution companies. These companies have their own range of career roles, from sales people to depot staff and management, etc.

Another function vital to the whole supply chain is logistics. This is more a precursor to distribution than part of it: it involves managing the flow of information within the supply chain. This means designing and managing the supply chain to ensure it runs as efficiently as possible, and then making changes to improve its efficiency further. Clearly, unless data is correct and available as needed, none of the processes described within this book are going to function properly.

PART THREE:
Getting into Retailing

Chapter 8
GETTING INTO RETAILING

This book describes retailing as an industry as well as working in retailing as a career. If you think that it might be for you, what do you do next? This section gives some tips and ideas for getting into your retailing career.

WORK EXPERIENCE

While at school

The best way to find out about any work is to do it. With retailing this is easy because shops are often on the lookout for people to work on a part-time basis. Most vacancies are for sales assistants or other entry-level work. Even if you're aiming for a career in buying or finance within retail rather than working directly with the public, you can still learn far more about retailing as an industry by doing a weekend or evening sales job than you ever will reading books about it. Part-time work like this also opens up future possibilities so always remember that the people you are working with could help you into a career job one day.

The large chains of retailers, department stores or other large organisations generally take part-time workers over the age of 16, so you may not be able to find work with them until your National Insurance number is issued to you. This should be just before your 16th birthday. Some, and smaller shops, might offer you work before this age but you need to ensure that this is legal: you are allowed to work a small number of hours each week below the age of 16, with your parents' or carers' permission. Make sure that you talk to them about this.

Think about the type of retailers that interest you and draw up a shortlist from visiting the high street, from the phone book and from the Internet. Think about what you will say to convince them that you are going to be a worthwhile member of staff. Remember that they are looking for staff who:

- always turn up, always on time
- are consistently cheerful and willing to do the work asked of them
- approach the work intelligently, wanting to learn
- have customer service skills already in place – an ability to have a polite conversation, to listen, respond, and so on. You won't need advanced sales skills but you will need to show you can talk to whoever you need to.

Remember, too, that they are more interested in workers who are planning to go into retailing as a career, as these are people who are more likely to want to learn and progress.

Make a shortlist of stores then phone around. They may send you an application form or may ask you to call in. When you call in, ask to see the person who recruits part-time staff. Think about your appearance and manner when you do this: you will want to give a good impression even at this stage, as you never know who you will meet. As with any application, fill in a photocopy of the form, review it and ask someone else to do this for you too, before sending off a final version. This might sound complex for a simple weekend job, but if you are interested in working for one of the large stores later on, perhaps as a management trainee after graduating, your early experience can make all the difference to getting a place. Later, when it comes to applying for management training courses, at least one store will have your work records available and will know that you are a diligent worker with great potential.

It could be useful to try working for a variety of different retailers: why not start as a newspaper-deliverer, then work behind the counter of the newsagency as you progress? Then maybe do Sundays in one of the large chains, as well as spending a vacation in a department store. You could try helping out down the market, too. This would give you a mix of different experiences and more of an overview of the retailing world. You need to ensure that you have a reasonable period of work in each of these, though: employers want workers who will stay for as long as possible as they invest in training you. Don't chop and change too often.

All work experience is important: you'll need details of it when applying for jobs in retailing later on. As you do the work, keep notes of the job titles, what you actually did and what you learned from it. You might like to keep these notes within your Record of Achievement folder when it's presented to you at the end of school year 11.

While at college

Students generally need vacation work to support themselves while they study. Most also have part-time work during term-time. If you are planning to do this and hope to go on to a career in retailing, then research your vacation/part-time work carefully. Think about which employers you might later apply to and try to get work in these or similar organisations.

There are other, more formal options. Some employers run schemes to get students involved in their organisations. These might be work placements arranged through the careers service at your college, or could be a 'year out' of a sandwich course, arranged through your department. The British Institute of Retailing (BIR) has a National Register of work placement opportunities – see their website for more information. You need to speak with your tutor or careers service staff to learn how to access these schemes.

Certainly, if you want to join a management training scheme when you graduate you'll need to show that you have a long-term commitment to retailing rather than just deciding at the last minute that you might fancy a job in a shop.

SPECIALIST COURSES

The chapter on qualifications (see page 19) looks at subjects you might study before starting a retailing career. Taking a relevant school or college course will help your application later on, though most work in retailing doesn't demand relevant study beforehand. Personal characteristics and experience are generally more important.

READING UP

Every industry has its own specialist or trade press. These are magazines/newspapers and more recently, websites read by professionals to support their work. They also carry recruitment advertising, which will help you understand job structures. You can learn a lot from them even if you don't understand it all. There are many specialist publications supporting the specialist arms of retailing such as grocery retailing. A good newsagent will have a listing of all available publications and will look through it with you (see Further Information page 89, for some title ideas). Alternatively, you can do an Internet search for publications. If you read this sort of publication over a period before making applications, your extended knowledge will come though and impress recruiters.

Also scan the financial pages of a daily newspaper to see what's happening on the business side of things: you'll be able to see which companies are making the largest profits, which are failing to attract customers, and so on.

Use the Internet as much as possible: a good starting point for topical retailing information is the British Retail Consortium (www.brc.org.uk).

NETWORKING

Talk to as many people in retailing as you can. These might be neighbours, people in shops – easily accessed! – or anyone else you bump into. Ask them about their work, what they like/dislike about it, what's happening within the industry and so on. You might also try junior commerce organisations. For instance, if you do business studies at school you'll get involved in an enterprise project, which might put you in touch with Chamber of Commerce or other local organisations. Try to attend events you hear about and again, speak with as many people there as possible. This builds your knowledge, and may provide useful contacts.

WHERE ELSE TO RESEARCH VACANCIES

Find out about job and training vacancies through the usual channels: your school or college careers service, your local authority careers service, your LSC (or regional variation – see Further Information page 86), vacancy publications, the Internet, contacts, and speculative applications.

APPLICATIONS

When to apply

Employers need people all the time but formal training schemes have set start dates. These are usually in the autumn after exam results come out and sometimes at intervals through the year. However, it could take a long time to get your job, so you need to be thinking about applying a good year before this date. If applications aren't due until later on, then you have at least done this basic research and can put the cut-off dates in your diary.

How to apply

Follow instructions. Make sure that you build on your work experience, pulling out the reasons for wanting to work in retailing from what you have learned as a sales assistant (or other role you may have performed).

If you're applying speculatively it's a good idea to telephone the recruitment department (or human resources, or personnel) to ask the best way to apply. Otherwise, a good, short but positive letter highlighting the reasons they will want to interview you, plus your CV, is best.

Interviews

Your application form/CV gets you into the interview room, but after that you need to present yourself persuasively. Do as much background research as possible. As with applying for part-time work (above), make sure you show off your customer service skills by communicating effectively. Generally, you won't need skills specific to retailing as the training will give you these, but you need to demonstrate as many personal skills as possible from the listing on page 16. Use details of your work experience to demonstrate these. Talk about issues relevant to retailing. And, as with any interview, use the opportunity to find out as much as possible about the organisation and training.

FINALLY

Retailing needs you. If initially you find it hard to get the place you're after, your determination will get you there, possibly by another route. If you give up and decide to try street-sweeping instead, well . . . perhaps you weren't cut out for a job in retailing after all. But if you're dynamic, motivated and look forward to moving fast through your career, then you'll have that pizzazz that'll get you the job. Good luck in your new career.

Chapter 9
FURTHER INFORMATION

British Institute of Retailing
First Floor, 1 Dean Street, London, W1V 5RN
Tel: 020 7495 1177

British Retail Consortium (BRC)
(Pressure group for the UK retail industry. The BRC is not geared up for training or careers information – any enquiries about these should go to other organisations.)
5 Grafton Street, London W1S 4EG
Tel: 020 7647 1500
www.brc.org.uk

Department for Education and Skills (DfES)
(For government information about education, training and skills.)

Sanctuary Buildings,
Great Smith Street,
London SW1P 3BT
Tel: 0870 000 2288
Website: www.dfes.gov.uk

Distributive Industries Training Advisery Council (DITAC)
(Provides information for employees and businesses in the retail and distributive trades.)
Middleton House, 2 Main Road,
Middleton Cheney, Banbury, OX17 2TN
Tel: 01295 712277
Website: www.di-net.org.uk

The Distributive National Training Organisation (DNTO)
(Develops and implements NVQs and other qualifications for the retail and distributive industries.)
Mardall House, 9–11 Vaughan Road,
Harpenden, AL5 4HU
Tel: 01582 760809
Website: www.dnto.com

DNTO has merged with the Hairdressing and Beauty Industry Authority (HABIA) to create a new Consumer Services body, ConServ. ConServ will apply to become a Sector Skills Council (SSC). Retailing will form a 'trailblazer' SSC. Trailblazers will demonstrate the value of strong and influential employer-led Sector Skills Councils and help develop effective ways of working for the first fully licensed SSCs that follow them. Search the DNTO website for developments.

Qualifications and Curriculum Authority (QCA)
('The Qualifications and Curriculum Authority brings together the work of the National Council for Vocational Qualifications (NCVQ) and the School Curriculum and Assessment Authority (SCAA) with additional powers and duties. This gives it a unique overview of curriculum, assessment and qualifications across the whole of education and training.')
Qualifications and Curriculum Authority,
83 Picadilly, London W1J 8QA
Tel: 020 7509 5555
Website: www.qca.org.uk

Scottish Qualifications Authority (SQA)
('The Scottish Qualifications Authority is the national body in Scotland for the development, accreditation, assessment, and certification of qualifications other than degrees.')
Hanover House, 24 Douglas Street, Glasgow G2 7NQ
Tel: 0141 248 7900
Website: www.sqa.org.uk

For information about training opportunities and employers, contact your local LSC (Learning and Skills Council) or TEC (Training and Enterprise Council), in England and Wales; LEC (Local Enterprise Company), in Scotland; or T and EA (Training and Enterprise Agency), in Northern Ireland. Find them in the phone book or ask your careers adviser.

AWARDING BODIES

You may never have direct contact with the bodies that develop and award your training qualifications as these will be organised through your employer or college. But if you want to do your own research you can contact them as follows:

City & Guilds
('C & G is the leading provider of vocational qualifications in the United Kingdom. Our qualifications and related services provide the means and motivation for individuals, corporations and communities to achieve their goals.')
City & Guilds of London Institute, Customer Services Enquiry Unit, 1 Giltspur Street,
London EC1A 9DD
Tel: 020 7294 2468
Website: www.city-and-guilds.co.uk

Edexcel
('Edexcel is one of the leading examining and awarding bodies in the UK and throughout the world providing a wide range of qualifications including GCSEs, GCE AS and A-levels; GNVQs, BTEC First, National, and Higher National Certificates and Diplomas; NVQs; Key Skills and Entry Qualifications and specific programmes for employers.')
Edexcel Foundation (incorporating BTEC)
Stewart House, 32 Russell Square, London WC1B 5DN
Tel: 0870 240 9800
Website: www.edexcel.org.uk

Oxford Cambridge and RSA Examinations
Westwood Way
Coventry CV4 8JQ
Tel: 02476 470033
Website: www.ocr.org.uk

UCAS (Universities and Colleges Admissions Service)
(For university entrance and information.)
Rose Hill, New Barn Lane, Cheltenham, Gloucestershire GL52 3LZ
Tel: 01242 227788
Website: www.ucas.com

SOME TRADE ORGANISATIONS REPRESENTING PARTICULAR INTERESTS

British Display Society
146 Welling Way, Kent DA16 2RS
Tel: 020 8856 2030
Website: www.messiterdesign.co.uk/bds/

British Franchise Association
Thames View, Newtown Road, Henley-on-Thames, Oxfordshire RG9
1HG
Tel: 01491 578049
Website: www.british-franchise.org.uk

Chartered Institute of Purchasing and Supply
Easton House, Easton on the Hill, Stamford, Lincolnshire PE9 3NZ
Tel: 01780 756777
Website: www.cips.org

Institute of Grocery Distribution
Grange Lane, Letchmore Heath, Watford, Hertfordshire WD25 8GD
Tel: 01923 857141
Website: www.igd.org.uk
www.careerchoices.org.uk – use this website for careers information
throughout the food and grocery industry, not just retailing.

National Federation of Retail Newsagents
Yeoman House, 11 Sekforde Street, Clerkenwell Green, London EC1R
0HA
Tel: 020 7253 4225
Website: www.nfrn.org.uk

Institute of Logistics and Transport
Supply Chain Centre, P O Box 5787, Corby,
Northants, NN17 4XQ
Tel: 01536 740100
www.iolt.org.uk

United Kingdom Warehousing Association
Walter House, 418-422 Strand, London WC2R 0PT
Tel: 020 7836 5522/0449
Website: www.ukwa.org.uk

Some more trade associations for Internet research

Association of Convenience Stores www.cstoreretailing.co.uk

British Hardware Federation www.bhfgroup.demon.co.uk

British Shops and Stores Association www.british-shops.co.uk

Electrical Distributors Association www.eda.org.uk

Hire Association Europe www.hae.org.uk

Institute of Customer Service NTO www.ics-nto.com

National Association of Funeral Directors email: info@nafd.org.uk
www.nafd.org.uk

National Association of Goldsmiths www.jewellers.org

National Pharmaceutical Association www.npa.co.uk

Radio, Electrical & Television Retailers' Association Ltd
www.retra.co.uk

Small Business Service www.businessadviceonline.org

Trading Standards Institute www.tradingstandards.gov.uk

FURTHER READING

Read the relevant trade newspapers and magazines to get an idea of what's going on in the areas that interest you. Some of these will be available at larger newsagents but all good newsagents will help you find and order the most appropriate journal for your interests.

Journals to look at include: *The Bookseller, CTN, Draper's Week, The Grocer, Retail Week*, etc.